Pg1.

SOLIDARITY CRY


Even today, I see social media posts about  [GWB] "Gardening while Black"; [MDHYWB] "My dog humped yours while Black"; [PTWB] "picking up trash while Black" (in your own neighborhood no less); and [TBPWB] "Taking Baby pictures while Black".  It would truly be comical if it weren't so insidious and extremely sad!!!  Once again, some random white person, calling the police on a random Black person in their vicinity.  We give them names like - [[Dog-Park-Diana]]. These names are out of frustration, but I'm sure they are also out of some coping mechanism that Black people (almost jokingly) use to try and make light of yet another offense to our collective community; whether we know the person or not!! And, to understand THAT sentiment, you have to look no further than Dr. Martin Luther King Jr. who was quoted as saying: "A threat to justice ANYWHERE, is a threat to justice EVERYWHERE!!"

It has been our (sometimes unconscious) "Solidarity cry", not merely because we are tired of these atrocities happening to OUR people, but we are tired of them, PERIOD!! And thus, our outcry, unbeknownst to our white counterpart... includes them.  I ask your immediate forgiveness, and If you will, I will assert this point from the very beginning of this book.  POINT: Black people do not have a major problem with including our white counterpart (again, if nowhere else, but in our subconscious) because we innately realize that - ALL PEOPLE CAME FROM US. Literally, ALL MANKIND came from us (or some person of color). We know that white people are just a lighter mutated DNA version of ourselves. Genetically speaking... we know that we can have children that "look white" - that's always been a

possibility. Also, alongside that notion, is our
arguably inherited / inbred 'coping mechanism' since
slavery 'til this very present day. This 'coping
mechanism' says, "that we must get along [with white
people] so as not to risk our lives".  I could
insert a lot of historical context here, but you
could also grab any movie in the past, recent
decades to see how or why that thought would be
played out. "Roots" by our famed Alex Haley -- told
his family story of STICKING TOGETHER even though,
they were still torn apart and devalued as any slave
would be. And then, to make my point even clearer,
followed up that acclaimed story with the authoring,
publishing, and (film) reproduction of the his
ancestor: "QUEEN" played by our gorgeous (mixed
race) African-American Oscar Winning Actress, Halle
Berry.  Berry's character was a light-skinned Black
woman whose troubled times not only centered around
the times in which she lived, but most immediately
centered around her skin complexion and how she
chose to represent herself against how she was
commonly expected to be treated during this
horrendous time.

And so, from the trunk of this proverbial tree
springs many branches that we will try to climb and
conquer - as we would hope is proper to pruning and
NOT towards demolishing what has been left of this
already decimated, yet still living, still fruit-
bearing, still worthy of our environmental care,
albeit twisted 'Americanized-tree-of-history'. -
Thus, so long as America stands beneath it,
representing its soil and its bedrock of existence
on this side of history, we will need to tend to
this poorly nourished tree. A tree stripped,
charred, replete with rope burns, waving its
American flag from its branches, and blood dripping
like exposed veins of sap, telling of  the forgotten
and/or neglected and purposefully omitted tales of
both internal and external abuse.

Moving forward, as we attempt to psycho-analyze
various bigoted social media content, please
understand that those will only represent 'the nose-
dive' as we look much, much further down into the

mind and behavioral patterns of white people and
Black people alike. It is not our initial intent to
bring discomfort, but understanding that discomfort
is EXACTLY what is needed to bring understanding and
healing.  Adults, we all learn to manage our
emotions and emotional states, as is fitting to us.
But we want to expose those as it relates to the
human subconscious, environmental triggers and past
educational points that those triggers may have been
exposed to. Most humans, at those of this current
age - should be able to tell you definitively that
"HATE is a learned behavior!!" No child comes out of
the womb with hate ingrained into themselves. Now, I
do believe there can be a form of evil that exists
in a child, but usually it is sparked as a result of
in utero trauma that is passed along through the
mother to the unborn child; conversely speaking,
which is usually the norm, women who suffer
traumatic events while pregnant, can produce
children who are victimized and perhaps overly
sensitive once they step foot into this world. It
can resemble a child born to a drug addicted mother,
but it shows up on the psychological / emotional
side of the scientific spectrum.

And so, we want you to consider, within the human
subconscious - there is a plethora of undefinable
experiences, stimuli, impulses, images, and more.
And while the subconscious is vastly underrated, it
controls a lot of what we do by way of conditioning.
This is where we want to focus a lot of our
attention in this book.

In fact, OUR Goal is to: Help you the reader,
regardless of your race, ethnicity, nationality,
however, discover and understand how your background
and upbringing influences how you interact and even
perceive African-American people of color. To this
end, we also anticipate more improved (race)
relations - and certainly more empathy as it relates
to people of color in and around your world.  For a
reader to deny these goals, means that you defiantly
choose to ignore that there is an option (another
option) or a solution. Those who choose to sidestep
these theories -  is like making yourself (once

again) part of the problem.  We sincerely hope that
this is NOT the case!!


FROM THE STANDPOINT OF HUMAN


Upon reading further, I do not want to make it
simple so as to gloss over the necessary mental
juggle - where we quickly grab whatever hat we feel
best fits and combats this subject matter - as if to
say... "See, I know all this already!!!"  Because
then, my response might immediately be to call you
an 'elitist' (which may or may not be true). But, I
need you to slow yourself down for a moment. Take a
beat. Take a breath!!

Right here, my job is to discover [whether you are
an alien or no??] = Or, is it safe to believe that
you were born of a woman, just like every other
HUMAN BEING??  That is my point to make!!  As a
human, you recognize - or, I am asking you to
recognize "yourself" -- long before your college
degrees, long before your political affiliation,
long before your opinions had a chance to sprout and
grow, and definitely before you started to add
accolades, attributes, and values to yourself and
those things attached to you, family included.
Before you knew what your name was - You were
human!! And I am a firm believer that THAT one
single, simple, point SHOULD be celebrated and
applauded. It's the one time where we are most
alike. But, I would imagine that even as I am
stating this - and you are reading this, you don't
or won't rest too long on that fact alone.  Your
mind (your conscious mind) says to you - "who are
you without all those things that make you
unique??!!" I bet that some people even find this
thought to be scary!!  This book is most definitely
FOR YOU.

We don't want to change who you are at your most
successful, fundamental level, ...but we are
absolutely going to ask you to IDENTIFY YOURSELF:

#1.) For yourself - and -
#2.) For the rest of us

I always say, "Nobody leaves planet earth UN-
checked" - and since you were not placed on this
planet alone, we are demanding a 'role call'.  HUMAN
is the first round of that role call. And we need
you to become intimately acquainted with what, who,
and why that is.  As a human (whether you believe
this or not) -- I assert that there is a certain
responsibility to and for every person who touches
the hallowed ground of this habitat.  Otherwise,
we'd gladly chuck you into the ocean, where you can
get acquainted with the fish!!  Of course, I'm
joking, but, look at how goofy that sounds!! And so,
If you had to define it, "what would you say is your
responsibility for being here, human???"  (Maybe we
can get you to write that down - so that we can
reference it later) - whatever you personally feel
that quest may be. Now, I don't really intend to
derive a whole spiritual movement from this
question, but if it moves you - it's worth taking
personal notice. How do you really feel about this
question?? This planet??  Yourself on this planet??

This is mainly conjecture and rhetoric for the sake
of filling the page of this book - but imagine
"HUMAN" means: "My human responsibility (before I
add anything else to it) is to figure out where the
sky touches the ground; Or, maybe to figure out how
long I can live under ground or under water; Or,
maybe to figure out why the other planets are spaced
so far apart from each other?? You could literally
make up anything here. It might even be a little
self-serving. But, as you can see, just to try and
answer that question alone TAKES SO MUCH OF YOUR
TIME AND THOUGHT PROCESSES. It's like - if you've
had the pleasure of vacationing all over the world.
where do we go next??  What is out there that we
haven't seen already?  Maybe a trip to outer space
IS the next destination?!!

But, per this page in the book, I regret to tell you
that -- OUTER SPACE is outta the question!!!  You
have not done your first work yet!  This book's

version of outer space requires a tax from you - and
it has nothing to do with your finances, your clout,
your prestige, your pedigree, your family name -
None of that!!  Instead, the one base question out
of several is: HOW HAVE YOU CONTRIBUTED to the
wellbeing of this planet (before we allow you to go
to space - and start wreaking havoc on everything
'out there'!!??  So many people would never get the
opportunity. We just have NOT yet done the necessary
earthly work in order to proclaim our collective
happiness here.

So, now that we've taken a moment to examine that
concept -- I want to start adding those things you
love about yourself - to yourself.  I must warn
though: Everything is going to be questioned.
Continue to read on.


From the state and position of human, you realize
that every person is exactly like every other person
-- and no, it does not matter if you have a
handicap, or your lifespan is one week. If you came
out of a womb, and you maintained your breathing for
a sustained period of time, and you have a brain
that aids you in development and function = HELLO
Ma'am / Sir, YOU ARE HUMAN!!  So, I would demand
that you stop treating yourself as if you were a
goose laying golden eggs!!  You're not.  You are
regular, and you are normal.  Basically human!!
That's all I want to declare.

Thankfully now, as we start to add various threads
to our individual life fabrics -- we rejoice. We
begin to rejoice in the fact that we are our
mother's children, our father son or daughter. We
love the fact that we grew up in Milwaukee,
Pensacola, Butte, Los Angeles, Waikiki,
Fredericksburg, Dover, New Orleans, Middleton, or
wherever you landed and grew up on this planet. That
specific area brought good times and bad times. You
weathered them all - and you  continued to move in
one direction or another - and you either [decided]
to stay or go to some other place that you felt was
more beneficial, likeable, suitable, and there were

no absolutes or guarantees.  I'm saying all this
just to paint the picture, and hopefully (here) you
can imagine how someone else may have had to contend
with some of the same things that may have come
quite easily to you; and vice versa, they may have
breezed through something that seemingly took you a
lifetime to figure out. So, there's no shame!!
Everyday, we decide that we are going to work on WHO
WE ARE - where we are!!

So enough of that. It is easily contestable that at
this very point is where we start to see the
struggle set in. Where your differences play a more
active role, and add shades of color to what used to
be (solid) Red, (pure) White, and (bold) Blue. But,
it is also here, where you start to point the
finger, and place blame - even as it relates to
those same colors. You feel justified. You feel
empowered or important. You couldn't handle another
existence, -- say, Mexico, or China!! - Heaven
forbid!! When it was all pure luck that you (the
mere human that you are) ended up HERE!!


MOTHERLAND


If you took the timeï¿½ beyond and between all the
yelling: "Go back to where you came from??!!" - you
would find that Black people, in particular, as it
relates to this statement, will fall into one of
several of the following categories:
#1.) We laugh at that statement, because we realize
- YOU are not from here either
#2.) We were removed from the very place that you're
trying to send us back to - and you really no longer
have any authority beyond that first trip.
#3.) We will gladly go back to where we came from -
I have a longing to be human there!!
#4.) We are not going ANYWHERE because THIS is my
home - and good luck trying to remove me from where
I stand
#5.) We recognize your self-hatred, even as you
continually try to push us away and downplay our

role in the development of what you so thoroughly
enjoy as a mutual citizen of this country. Stop
lying to yourself!!
#6.) We are oh so very tired of all these tirades
and tantrums - please, oh pleaseï¿½ learn respect
and appreciation before things start getting real
around here; the smile is starting to fade!!
#7.) We realize that there is a real fear - because
as the future moves toward us, you will be readily,
quickly, smoothly and effectively displaced as a
white [so-called] majority.

It's important that you know these facts, because to
vocalize so many (what might seem to be hurtful)
ramblings and rants, only force the idea that
clearly - there is something wrong with you!!
Actually, I am of the opinion that many white people
believe that Black people also hold all these secret
prejudices against them too. Which is actually, not
that true. By and large, if you ever got close
enough, you'd find that most Black people do not
have a secret word that they call white people.
But, if there were oneï¿½ it would probably be
"EVIL"!!  To which you probably privately retort and
self-question, "if that's trueï¿½ why am I reading
this bookï¿½. Seeing how Black people view me?? How
dare they call white people, evil?!!"

Notice I am laying a path and setting up a narrative
that will be tackled later in this book. For now,
all these things are being presented so that we have
several things to view as we move forward regarding
this subject of white fragility. So, as we step very
gingerly in that direction, I must declare another
eye-opening truth or two.  And, here it is: Black
people do not feel the need to become "white"!!  To
a Black person, dependent upon the hordes of people
you could ask over a long period of timeï¿½. To a
Black person, "white" might mean some version of
"economics"; or maybe it means "education". But it
does not ever mean "loss of identity, culture or
color".  With this, you can think of someone who
loves Elvis. As a singer, they may VIEW Elvis as
"the vest there ever was"!!  They may love his movie
appearances. They may love his style and flair as a

performerï¿½. ESPECIALLY, If Elvis were the only
person they'd ever seen after those various artistic
manners. To point: No one is TRYING to become Elvis
- it (his music) is just a point of appreciation for
a Black man who is regarding this icon. The two
actually seem diametrically opposed to one another -
even and especially considering that Elvis received
(stole) a lot of his moves from the very talented
Black people of his generation.

Another truth to shed light upon us is this: Black
people do not need to apologize for your
discomfortï¿½.. That's basically a form of slavery
PTSD for white people. Hence, the subject of this
book: white fragility. Please understand - therein
lies the healing that you seek; and your discomfort
is a prerequisite and a requirement. School is now
in session!!  At some point, you will begin to ask
yourselfï¿½. "Who is your 'trusted' Black person in
your life that you can talk to??"  If you feel you
do not have oneï¿½. Wellï¿½. Let's get the lesson
started.




THE SUBCONSCIOUS MIND - ROLES REVEALED


All of life is a classroom. What (by comparison) are
you trying to learn vs. the things that you have
learned in the past??  Are you maintaining your life
based upon things you decided were good and right
for you - as a child; such as "I'm going to eat ice
cream everyday for dinner".  I'm sure most of that
has changed with your newly advanced maturity. The
roles that we play - CHANGE.  They must, they have
toï¿½. And so, we seek out moments, events, and
people, or relationships that best support the new
role and directions we have adapted for ourselves.
Consider this: Whether you are going to church, or
going to a department store - you encounter someone
who will give you insight or assistance. At church,
you have the pastor (or priest) delivering a message
that inspires you, while at a department store, you
will inevitably walk over to a counter/clerk/expert

who can help you or direct you towards the thing you seek. So, I askï¿½. Why would you NOT have the same regarding racial issues???

No doubt, white fragility has kept you from achieving this very, very minor goal, and it is a necessary component for your life. It says a lot about you if, in fact, you do not have any direct connections or have a distinct fear of approaching a person of color - even for the purpose of learning and/or expanding yourself.

To never have thought of, approached, or found a person of color with whom you can have a (potentially close) relationship with signifies that you have an extremely deep-seated and deep-seeded self-hatred, which may carry an overlay of superiority, or victimhood, or anything that causes (what I will call:) 'Racial Alienation'. It's as if you walk out of your house, and go to a job (or anywhere) where you somehow believe - only white people (should) exist.  Subconsciously, you may have trained yourself to think that - even thoughï¿½ obviously, to walk out of your front door, you immediately see other races, all kinds of ethnicities moving about and living their lives. Although, it is possibleï¿½ In extreme cases like a cult, or letï¿½s say, an Amish communityï¿½. You may not IMMEDIATELY see others (races), but you know they exist. Henceï¿½ The idea that you can somehow convincingly disconnect yourself from another race or other races becomes ludicrous.  Somewhere in your subconscious mind, you have fabricated a lieï¿½ that is enforced daily. The subconscious does not REACT to this information like it's a lieï¿½ it merely plays the reel-to-reel that this is your experience. This is your experience (as you see it or wish it), but it is NOT real or true.

The subconscious mind (without judgement) records everything. It records, for example, a moment where - you see THE AFFECTS of something that you wanted or not wanted, and where you consciously (almost audibly) yell - BINGO!! The subconscious saysï¿½ "WHOA, they really felt that oneï¿½.. Look at that

beautiful emotional flare / fire / spark my owner
has created right now!!  How can we get more of
that!!??" - That's all the subconscious does -
initially.

We want to create more of those - WHOA momentsï¿½.
But we must filter out the foolishness which eludes
or excludes people. The people, per se, are not your
goalï¿½. They help to increase the FLARE. How
effective is a match as compared to a bonfire when
you're trying to stay warm??

By NOT having a person of color in your lifeï¿½ you
lessen your flare experiences and moments.  If I can
point it out this way, it is exactly why we have the
argument of 'cultural appropriation' - where many
white people actually love Black music, love Black
genitalia, maybe love Black food (or create
stereotypes surrounding), and maybe unconsciously
love Black swagger / sex appeal / mystique. By NOT
having a person of color in your lifeï¿½. You
immediately [GET IT WRONG] because your seemingly
inappropriate love affair or segmented interest is
NOT TIED to anything.  Of course, you can enjoy East
Indian food or Chinese food without being tied to,
or connected to anyone from those places /
regionsï¿½. But, YOU CANNOT comment on it,
intelligently. If you are not connected to that
culture or those people, ï¿½ you are just passing
thru - and you may be breaking the speed limit
and/or a lot of rules of respect and appreciation.
If your goal is to INCREASE THE FLARE, you have to
at the very least, plan a day-trip (so-to-speak).
You do not gain the understanding - which you should
already haveï¿½ thatï¿½. without Black people, YOU
would not be possible; you would NOT exist.

Of course, you can exist without the knowledge that
you emerge from a person of color, ï¿½.but you make
it more difficult to love yourself, hence more
difficult to love others [period]. The FLARE that
your subconscious desires is - I LOVE MEï¿½. And I
LOVE SO MUCH of the things about you that make you
similar to me / having things in common with me. The
FLARE that you unwittingly create (without this

knowledge) gives off the adverse vibe - sent from
your subconscious - that others don't matter or are
inferior. You can absolutely live your whole life
that way ï¿½ but I consider that, unevolved, at
best. You can NEVER truly evolve.  WHY?? Because,
ï¿½Hatred blocks evolution!!

So, with the subconscious mindï¿½. Let's try a quick
experiment:
If I ask you to pull up a video on YouTube (or
simply recall, if you can), the song: "Baby Shark"
(which I love and quickly  makes me smile every time
I hear it!!) - and upon seeing / hearing that
songï¿½. Try to continue reading this book / these
surrounding pages WITHOUT that song interfering. It
may prove impossible to some.  We've all had those
moments where we hear a song, and it never leaves
our brainsï¿½ it just keeps playing!! Songs like:
Tom's Diner, or Taylor Swift's "Shake it off" are
infectious, They are flukes of nature - and many
people have absorbed those songs into their
subconscious as a matchlike flare - that brings a
smile or a spark of joy, or maybe it causes trauma
because that's how you personally related to that
song - like someone who was locked in a prison and
forced to listen to that one song, over and over and
over, for days and weeks on-end!! It may represent
death. To make my point:

1.  Mark any feelings that this song has pulled
    forward in you / your mind / your heart.
2.  Understand that this feeling marks your
    subconscious at work (if this applies),
    nowï¿½turn off the song.
3.  Are you still thinking or humming the song
    (while you read these lines and pages)??
4.  NOWï¿½. Consider your worst image, idea, or
    story about a person of color: what happened??
5.  Does the feeling mix or change - and become
    different??  It's telling the depths of your
    hatred subconsciously.
6.  Notice how the song still prevails - in most
    cases - and/or whether the hatred has taken
    over.

7.  Now, it all blursï¿½. Depending upon what your
    active brain THINKS NEXTï¿½. Oh, my food is
    burning!!
8.  IF YOU CAN, pull yourself back to the song and
    think something good or amazing about a
    person/people of color.
9.  If that new thought can make you smile as much
    or more as the song doesï¿½. Voila!! You are 1
    step ON the path.
10.  Music is powerful and we can mark our 'FLARE
     moments' with an appropriate song / food /
     conversation / etc.

Your immediate resistance to new things, and your
'learned resistance' to life, people, events, and
certain emotions proves that your brain and muscle
reflexes are under an attack called: stress. So,
just being aware at that level is important -
because otherwise, we would not know what it is we
are looking for within ourselves. What needs to
change. And this barely touches the above paragraphs
because, for example, we can have stress and know
that we need to lose weight - which is causing us
stressï¿½. But it is much, much, much different from
the stress of hatred that lives inside of us, dries
out our skin over ages, generations, timespans of
years, emotionally and psychologically. It's like a
dormant curse!!  But, it's NOT dormant at all.

This is why we MUST, MUST look at these deep-seated
and deep-seeded things. We MUST, MUST be willing to
face them - as scary as they may be. And mind you,
they will be YOUR OWN PERSONAL KIND OF SCARYï¿½ not
mine. It will wear the mask that most affects you,
for you were the original creator of that self-same
mask. ï¿½Profound, yes??!! Were you intending to
"scare yourself 'til death"??  Facing those things
must use the courage of your egoï¿½ to tell your
(own) egoï¿½. Back off, I'm going to take the wheel
for a moment!!  There WILL BE an emotion / emotional
response.

You OWN your subconsciousness, your subconsciousness
DOES NOT own you. Therefore, you must OWN YOUR
(emotional or not) BELIEFS' outcomes, and not foist

them onto othersï¿½.. In this moment or in general.
Thus, you really DON'T HATE Black people. But, you
DO need to turn that white fragility clause deed
down inside of you into something:
A)   Useful
B)   NOT fear related
C)   Something that is NOT temporal - like eating a
     meal (that you digest to produce waste)
D)   Live out its ENHANCEMENT as health (just like a
     meal that you digest to feed your blood stream)

Even while writing this book, as a Black man, I am
subtly, and almost unconsciously confronting my own
diet and ideologies about white people - which (not
speaking in a diminishing fashion) means NOT a lot,
because I have pretty healthy relationships with
white people; as many Black people do.  But what I
confront is the "EVIL" that I feel exists inside of
certain kinds of white people who feel its okay and
even convenient for them to interrupt my life with
their white hatred foolishness; THAT PARTï¿½ IS VERY
REAL.

Most Black people sort of say to themselves: Don't
start noneï¿½. Won't be none!!! And to the average
white person, that statement means absolutely zero,
other than the fact that they can read and
understand the order of words. Black people
implicitly understand what I mean when I say that -
written or spoken!! Anyone who has lived outside of
the black culture, for example, will not clearly
hear, nor understand why Black people might say, "By
any means necessary". Outside of the culture, one
would only relate this comment back to something the
very Black and militant (aka - white word for:
dangerous) political rights activist, Malcom X once
used as a quote.  Mind you, outside of the culture
in some of these instances, is the correct place to
be.  Foisting your FEAR of that person, that
statement, that era of hatred, that "us vs. them"
angstï¿½ is DEFIANTLY WRONG - and yes, outside of
the culture.

AND SO - My writing allows me to visit the present,
the past (history) and social / societal injuries

that I've experienced (as a Black man), and
brilliantly allows me to analyze functional
philosophies - from an heightened (maybe elevated)
post. I can imagine someone turning my last words
into 'superiority' or 'arrogance' - which would be
incorrect. Mainly because, I understand that being
able to detach oneself from internal things (AFTER
they've brought them to the light and found healing
resolution) makes for careful objectification and
insight which points directly to wisdom. In other
words, my experience writing this book, affords me
many rebirths, affirms who I already know I am as a
black man, and in the most non-judgmental form or
fashion, opens the way for pure healing to those
non-black readers grappling with these printed
words; they become 'spirit' for you, not just some
random, rambling, complaint session.

As I have found what triggers me most - I can now
say that understanding that "my subconscious mind is
responsible for various necessary pointsï¿½ like
self-motivation". The subconscious is not a waster
of time, thusï¿½ it is extremely, extremely adept
and efficient (like the many computer analogies
that are use to describe). Since my youth until now,
I have always hated to waste my time. I am very
result-orientedï¿½. But, I'm also very, very, very
intuitive (and feel that one of these have always
had to suffer against the other, over life's years -
which I have now learned is not really accurate or
true). So, to take advantage of my time
fraudulently, waste my time or energy, or to feed
that perception is completely unhealthy for me. What
is my subconscious trying to doï¿½ what FLARES have
I fed it (by being angry when a result was not
produced, as I imagined it)?? This sounds like the
same hatred that might come from a seemingly futile
encounter with a Black person - which has nothing to
do with the make-up or existence, or overall persona
of that person (of color or otherwise). Like me,
now, one might be willing to say - that 'flare' had
everything to do with ME alone.

When our subconscious is motivating usï¿½ your
emotions look like sign posts: MERGE, YIELD, STOP,

PROCEED WITH CAUTION. Let's use peer pressure as an exampleï¿½. Which is really truly a loophole - to understanding our growing selves and the things we deem as important, how and when we learned those may be here!!

With peer pressure (the mostly negative version), we start to look almost completely outwardly - as it relates to our immediate world, as we wear what's fashionable per our friends, tv, and mags, and then we make out our social calendars according to the same. We learn or discover that we need to drink to be accepted, attend parties to be accepted and/or deemed as popular, and we rebel against the things that were emotionally, psychologically given to us as a child. If you are a strong person, at the very least, you may pause for a moment or say, "No thanks!! My family would not approve!!" Soï¿½. What is motivating our behavior during this time of our lives??? Why do we NOT put off these things - like sex or drugs, until we are responsible and consenting adults. Society and the subconscious portray themselves to be working together to make one well-rounded or worldly. Andï¿½.. Subjectively (and subconsciously speaking), one may go through these things and still be okay towards becoming a constructive, productive adult. These experiences do NOT have to lead to ruin. But, that's on the surfaceï¿½. What was the FLARE that you produced?? You sayï¿½ "WHOA, I really like drugs!!" - and you have altered the existence of that sweet little boy / girl who was birthed in love and peaceï¿½ and added, what is arguably - the most unnecessary component that is reshaping your life forever. So, is your subconscious NOW motivating you to drink??

This is (then) the section where we try to conquer or understand "habitual thinking"ï¿½. Habitual thinking being that distinct difference between - the subconscious on Autopilot: "I'm going to bake a cake" vs. the very active and very Conscious mind: The world of "my food is burning!!"  As with the active thought life, we DECIDE to do this or that. The subconscious mind is more like THIS:  When

someone asks you - How was your day?? -or- What did
you think of the movie?? We search ourselves in a
millisecond to respond with feelings, and emotions,
and comparisons to other pictures, moments, and
eventsï¿½. depending upon whether we are trying to
influence "the funny side", or "the thought-
provoking intelligent side", or "the THIS memory is
similar to OUR / THAT last memory" -- our answer
takes on many shades. The shades help to influence
how we move or are perceived by others moving around
us.

When you were a childï¿½ you spoke as one. And, if
someone asked you your nameï¿½. as a child,
somewhere, you heard a seemingly cute / curt
statement and you respond with, "Puddin'tain, ask me
again and I'll tell you the same!!"  (you might [do]
that response several times without thinking).  That
reply is set subconsciously. Then, one day (usually
subconsciously), you no longer find it appropriate
to answer in that manner. The reason is: you've
matured subconsciously), you want to give a good
impression to a person you like or respect (and I'm
going to say "subconsciously" to all of the
following examples). You have changed how you decide
to move thru the world - and how you now choose to
present yourself to others, you learn the love and
power of your own name, you encountered an
unfavorable retort - which made you feel badlyï¿½.
And we can go on ad infinitum. Subconsciously,
something was triggeredï¿½. Like, let's say, you
said that childish remark to an adult in front of
your mother and she scolded you; and so, maybe with
a few tearsï¿½. You stopped COLD. You packed it
away, and never said it again!!  None of this is
really an active thought - other than it was the
fact that you were [going through] experiencing a
new, sizeable moment that was not pre-planned or
maybe even expected.  The egoic INSTRUCTIONS TO THE
FLARE were - don't do that, do this instead!

With active thought, we decide to get up when
someone knocks at the door. It can be automatic in a
very small sense, but we sayï¿½"Oh, someone is
there! Who is it?! (in our mind)" and we MOVE - we

don't have to consult our muscle, and whether they
are readyï¿½ we burst into motion - our active mind.
When people are talking to usï¿½. We choose to be
ACTIVE and listen to every single word they are
speaking, or our subconscious may take over and we
drift off into a daydream, even though we are still
[quote-end quote] "listening!!" As you can seeï¿½
there's a thin line between these two, but with very
different, and sometimes obvious differences in
function.  But, the one thing you want to
continually remind yourself is that the subconscious
is always seeking the best of your joy and
healingï¿½.. IT never ever hurts (in theory)ï¿½. It
only REACTS // REACTS ONLY.

This is why it is so critical for us to understand
and know HOW we feed our subconscious / perceptions.
When you go into the refrigerator, you see a jug of
milkï¿½ HOW LONG has it been there??? Is it
spoiled??  Your conscious will just drink (and end
up spitting out the spoiled milk, if in fact it is
"perceived" as such)ï¿½. But the subconscious mind
will automatically say (in order to answer the
spoiled milk question), "you know what, let me smell
it first!!"

Soï¿½. Let's now delve into our subconscious as it
perceives the things, people, events, and constant
data floating around us every moment of every day.
You have two earsï¿½. Do you have a shut-off knob
for them??  The human answer is, No. And so with the
brainï¿½ it is the same. Our subconscious creates a
collage of unexplainable images and picturesï¿½..
Some are important and some are not meaningful at
all, but they support another thought or idea. You
can have a collage of an apple (which is the most
important object, the theme of the collage), but the
theme is better understood against other apples, or
even better yetï¿½ a insignificant and seemingly
meaningless image of an apple tree.  Is there one
apple on that tree or many apples on that tree??
These weave the meaning into the image and support
the universal idea that apples come from / grow on
trees.

Now, let's take that same appleï¿½ï¿½ and place it
next to the image of a woman's vagina; what is the
derived meaning???
If those are the only two images, you basically make
up a story; right??!!??  If I add a bench, and a
skyscraper in the background next to this naked
woman, and then I add an upside down spilled ice
cream cone (strawberry) on the ground in front of
herï¿½.. What is the collage trying to tell us
now???  We have no clue!! We think it's strange or
bizarre or meaningless and useless.  Wellï¿½ this is
our subconscious mind trying to make sense of all
the gazillion things that go on around us daily -
even without much active thought being inserted.
For the sake of understanding white fragility, we
will make this strangely virile collage to represent
our inheritance from our family background [noise].
This poorly inherited white DNA, filled with hatred
for people of color, actually does move forward
within usï¿½.. We try to deny it or remove it from
history, but the collage CANNOT BE UN-MADE.  It has
become apart of our fabric. It has become one of the
famed portraits that hang in our 'psychological
family home' - just like Uncle Willie.

When the subconscious is following orders
(instinctually, of course)ï¿½.. It is devoid of
'racial judgments' good or bad, because it does not
react - to sayï¿½. Oh no!! Don't say that!!  -or-
"Oh no, wearing Blackface is bad and extremely
culturally inappropriate!!" - those things are
decided at some point by the conscious mind, first.

'Conscious hatred' produces a lifetime of
resultsï¿½ï¿½ fights break out, words are hurled,
racial slurs are fully charged, anger and other
emotions are stirred, 'flares' are waiting to be
triggered into a later belief.  THE BIG QUESTION is:
who's doing the hatingï¿½. Your past (self /
subconscious / family subconscious), your mind
(active / in the moment / using an outdated collage
/ new expression), or you (unevolved self-hatred /
culturally disconnected quasi-human brain)??  If you
are a body first, type of personï¿½.. You are only
getting queues from the immediate world around you;

you are gullible and have no depth of personal
understanding.  We do, however, experience the world
with our body firstï¿½ but, it is with our
understanding of ourselves that we then CREATE the
outer world around us, ï¿½.secondly.

So, it is because of this that we ask: What's your
DEEP (subconscious) MOTIVATIONï¿½..???  Realizing
that we are speaking about that 95% portion of
yourself; your subconscious. What's the motivation
for hate within you??  What's the motivation for
FEAR within you??  Why are you choosing to vomit all
of that (personal stuff) onto Black people??  Let's
pause and really think about those questionsï¿½
maybe glance back at the statement we requested that
you write down at the beginning of this book. Is
there a difference between what you wrote and what
you feel as an adequate, reasonable answer to these
questions?

Research again, your BELIEFS about Black
peopleï¿½ï¿½. Close your eyes and think about black
people all around you; what are they doing? Describe
what they look like?? What are they wearing??  Is
this your imagination or do the thoughts naturally
come up from someplace else inside of you?? Does
these thoughts support the strange naked collage we
talked aboutï¿½ or have you had an opportunity to
see the Black father coming home from work, greeting
his children with kisses and hugs, go inside to
prepare themselves for dinner at the dining room
table as his wife quickly finishes cooking the meal
and setting the table - after greeting her husband
safely home from the big bad cruel world outside.
She kisses him in triumphant protest of his arrival
back home!!  Is that the kind of picture you see in
your mind??  Write down the differencesï¿½ this is
VERY, VERY, VERY IMPORTANT!!

Your bleak version, however accurate you may feel
that version may be, is solely based upon whatever
you have allowed this world to feed you about Black
people, or what you have purposefully fed yourself.
There's no other two ways about it. Whether
historical inaccuracies, historical lies, whether

crimes committed, murders that were executed
directly or indirectly, whether movie images you've
absorbed and believed to represent something
realiï¿½. However, whatever. The one of two ways or
both together -- paint the most shocking picture of
how you have unlovingly held Black people, in the
name of white fragility or otherwise.  Your
subconscious mind is awaiting NEW instructions to
better express the truth of who you are inside of
your own subconscious realms.  So, let's quickly
recap:

Your subconscious mind:
Does not chooseï¿½ only reactsï¿½..  If you are
dying of thirst/ dehydratedï¿½. Your subconscious
triggers a water search.
Your active mind tells you where to go - based upon
the closest water source: lake, refrigerator, store,
or hospital.

Does not chooseï¿½ only reactsï¿½..  If you are
having a dreamï¿½.. Your subconscious triggers your
body's blood flow / sweat / muscle movement in order
to keep you cool or calm, or alerts you to get ready
to fight.
Your active mind wakes you up, and using your eyes
tells you that you were NOT in this "waking
reality".

Does not chooseï¿½ only reactsï¿½..  If you are
watching a scary movieï¿½.. Your subconscious body
flinches / head turns / closes your eyes / balls up
fist or whatever you've trained yourself to believe
about scary movies.
Your active mind laughs and dismisses the moment as
not real; you take a sip of your beverage, or eat
some popcorn.

Does not chooseï¿½ only reactsï¿½.   If you
encounter a situation that causes anxiety (which is
never a reality, only a perception of what you call
'anxiety')ï¿½. In your subconscious
(psychologically), you react with anxiety (a mask
you created) and wonder whether you will fail the
test, or not be able to sing publicly, or shrink as

if you seem stupid or unknowledgeable as a 1st try -
and will make you feel you want to run away.
Your active mind tells you to leave, or it tells you
to quit, or it makes an excuse to spout aloud to
cover embarrassment.

Does not chooseï¿½ only reactsï¿½.   If you have a
human body, your body health works
automaticallyï¿½.. It works without your help or
active (do it now) permission.
Your active mind may say, "I feel like going / I am
going to the gym".ï¿½ in support of that perceived
health.

Does not chooseï¿½ only reactsï¿½.   If you learn /
teach yourself to ["see good"] and approach Black
people about / with that [good you see]ï¿½ï¿½ Your
subconscious mind will store that until it becomes a
belief.
Your active mind should then lead you to seek out
[MORE} of that very same [good you see] in Black
people. Then, you can walk up and start a
conversation by giving yourself into a compliment or
however, and show lots of respect and appreciation
directly to that Black person you are speaking with.
EXAMPLE:  "Excuse me, I noticed that watch you are
wearing, I saw one just like itï¿½. That looks good
on you!! Now, (you make me wish) I wish that I
wasn't afraid to spend the money on a new watch!  My
name is ï¿½.. ?? (pause)  What's your name??  [HUMAN
FIRST} ï¿½you can ask him about being black LATER

So now we see that, the subconscious mind:
*   represents about 95% of who we are and how we
    think
*   represents our body and other functions in an
    AUTOPILOT type of manner; it only reacts.
*   does not ask for permission, but does follow
    active mind instructions - as it relates to our
    whole being.
*   functions off of "perceptions" and stored data,
    images, and experiences since our birth until
    right now.
*   controls our emotions and those emotions over
    time become our beliefs.

* triggers dreams and body language & muscle
  responses
* responsible for love, hate, and our EVERY
  motivation behind our desires, our best life, and
  healing.
* emotions act as a sign to what is IMPORTANT. If
  you are having an emotion, you are an "affected
  being"; LISTEN!
* does not waste time, and does not inspire wasting
  time.

I caution you:  Be upfront later down the road, and
let this new Black friend know that you are
["SEEKING GROWTH" and want to learn more about "what
it means to be Black in America / the world"]. Let
them know that you would love to get their insight,
as a trusted friend, if you ever have a question
about race.  Being abrupt and talking about on-the-
spot Black discussions ARE very doableï¿½. But will
lack a tiny bit of intimate insight and humanness.
Start with, "Hey can I ask you a question about
race, I'm trying to learnï¿½ï¿½????? (how a Black
man or woman feels / thinks) aboutï¿½..[subject]???"
Be prepared for any responseï¿½. And it may not be
personal, but it may be blunt.  Usually, people want
to know why you are asking them about something so
personal.  Thanks to racism, some scars never
properly heal!!


LET'S TACKLE RACISM


You may have heard it voiced a time or two - how
that one might feel (white people might feel) that,
"Racism is IN THE PAST and Black people should just
get over it already!!" -- but much like the Jewish
holocaust, the ill treatment of Black people has
become an almost celebrated moment - where we say,
"THIS WILL NEVER HAPPEN TO US AGAIN!!" And
certainly, no one would blame a holocaust victim for
declaring such a stance. And soï¿½. Whether
personally or collectively - the wounds may still be
present, the scars forever visible, and the pain

like a phantom limb still aching and throbbing with actual, living, very real pain. So, when we consider a human's subjective perspective on very personal (and seemingly trite) landmark moments - that may not have befallen them personally, but actually DID occur to their grandparents, or howeverï¿½. Understand, the depths of what you see as surpassable and surmountable, has become a 30 foot tall blockade that's 50 years wide. There is not much getting around it.  Hence, we will tackle 'Racism' - and where you might find yourself within or prayerfully, without.

Let's assume the above 'Black friendship'; has been newly achieved. You still have no idea what to expect. Well, let me paint that very vivid scenario for you. Racism is like a university college campus. "ï¿½Say what??!!" - you say!!  Yes. Imagine a college campus that has 10 buildings, all surrounding the main administration building that contains the student union, the admissions offices, and the bursar's office where you gladly pay your money every semester or quarter. It's the main hubï¿½. Replete with cafes, restaurants, study halls, entertainment and more.

Building #1: Let's call it - The Department of Psychology!! As you may imagine, the professors there are ripe with controversy, and steamy dialogues that sparks great theoretical debates. Racism as a psychology - again, involving the subconscious hereï¿½. Has been a very hallowed hall of opinions, thoughts, and basic rhetoric that touches back to its philosophical forefathers: The KKK, Slave Traders, Presidents and rulers, and of course, let's not forget Hitler. I'm sure we could name more, but you see my point. For centuries (it seems), and definitely since the dawn of the Americas, we have purported that freedom was this valuable, abundant, commodity - available to everyone. But, everyoneï¿½ was not even considered 'human'. Some of those everyone's were considered 'less-than-human chattel' - which doubled as wealth. So, where does that idea stem from?? I'm asking a rhetorical question here becauseï¿½. If we really

knew, or there were ONE PARTICULAR PERSON to
blameï¿½. We might be able to go back and overturn
that thought with right actions.  But as it
standsï¿½ especially as it relates to any
philosophy, there was a GROUP MENTALITY that chose
to adapt this plan into an actionable event. As a
Black man, I'm sure that I am fairly safe in saying
that there (probably) weren't very many Black men
who were apart of this group mentality. And soï¿½
the separation of white and Black begins - or is
more pronounced as it related to one's philosophy,
potential policy, and desired wealth status.  The
psychology necessary for one to employ racism -
requires a degree from this prestigious college:
White, Wealthy, and "Willing to die" for this
fraternity of geniuses - whose greed was paramount
against all else; sometimes against other whites who
did not measure up.

It leads us to a discussion of ethics, how thatï¿½
if I own a plantation - how should it be run, or if
I own a business - whom should it benefit and
service?? If one can find a way to include or
exclude "undesirables" or "people from shithole
countries", than we can boost our monies, our power,
our prowess, or our manufactured philosophy to
others who will 'do us good'.  This growing group
all pressing towards this Elysium-like state of
clever, superior, Euphoria.

Psychologically, since most of the brown people
walking around on the earth were intentionally
OUSTED from any possibility of taking advantage of
this advantage, it leaves very little to wonder why
certain segments of the world, let alone the United
States, suffers such great pangs of poverty. Whether
you're looking to Mexico, or Africa, or whereverï¿½
you see the thread of this psychology tautly running
just below the surface of the mainstream. Tightly
held knowledge, tightly held opportunities - later
named Yale, and Harvard, and the like, tightly held
words of appreciation for those who would make you
richer and richer for very little or zero pay -
these mind games served their double-minded purpose
very effectively; even until this very day. So, I

askï¿½. Where do you see yourself?? It begs the question to ask such a poignant query given the fact that white fragility seems to provoke internally, some sort of discomfort at the documented and obvious facts that - in this country alone - there was insidiously created a system that sought to cast out and/or separate peoples for the sake of monetary gain via collective thought. For example: Have you ever received an inheritance? Have you ever visited a plot of land or property that was owned or passed down by your family? Are you whiteï¿½ and maybe even, are you an offspring of an alumni to any college (or a prestigious university)?? Just to assume these questions places you (almost) squarely within the highest debates of this department. You may feel it's unfair to say so - but, when you consider that people of color could not freely earn, could not attend any college, could not find themselves on the level and even playing field of this very recent time in young America's existenceï¿½ then you see what damage could have easily been dealt or further cultivated, had not Black people had the one or two Philosophical-like leaders that come to mind: Dr. Martin Luther King Jr. and the honorable activist, Malcolm X. ï¿½.Mind you, both of these men, powerful in their own rights, serve as statues to the Department of Psychology's success (per se) - Malcolm X never attended college and barely attended high schoolï¿½. While his more peace-loving counterpart attended and graduated from a Historically Black College in 1948. This, and other Historically Black Colleges and Universities, were birthed due to the fact that we were still being denied education - well beyond the ratification that ended slavery on January 31st, 1865; unless you're talking about Mississippi, of course.

There is no tool to measure the psychological impact of slavery and/or racism over the past decades. One can only look at the advancements of individuals, and in some cases, agencies or corporations that were created by people of color. And even still - these serve as the exception, rather than the standard. We still have Black people TODAY, who, if

they attend collegeï¿½ may be the first ones in
their whole entire family to do so. Soï¿½. We
applaud the very calculated damage that not only
slavery produced, but those forefathers who sought
to separate for themselves, a life and a lifestyle
that would later afford them - EASE!!  This is the
underbelly of racismï¿½ it is not an obvious point
of reference. Albeit negative, given the chance to
research your grandfather, or your grandfather's
father, you could reveal something that has been
passed down to you - which causes you to feel this
white fragility. And you should never downplay it.
Itï¿½s there for a reason. But, as you continue to
feed yourself along this book's dialogue ï¿½ Healing
ensues.

When you consider that, aside from research, a lot
of this information that I am writing / creating is
flowing FROM my subconscious, the question of what
one should feed themselves is the actual,
figurative, fork in the road for many people of
color who have not (yet and still) had the chance to
have 'college-without-racism' modeled for them. The
money alone stands as a huge obstacle, when they
innately understand that mommy and daddy need that
money to pay the rent, take care of everyone, and
maybe breathe once or twice. So, the Department of
Psychology for a Black man all but does not exist -
unless you've learned to feed yourself well,
psychologically. Since it was denied to us, we often
side with the grit and the grind of every day life -
to teach us. We've continued to "survive", and so we
have made that survival our diploma, our degree, our
journey, and our graduation in death.  Changing that
type of psychology and/or philosophy will take a few
more generations with extreme, concentrated, effort
- to rid.


Building #2: Let's call it - The Department of
Ethics and Business Practices!!
As I've quickly touched upon it ï¿½ within a few
other nuance items slid in, as well; The Department
of Ethics speaks to our business practices, and NOT
just in the form of making money. As a fast example:

When you hear that 'Shantae' was denied an interview
for a job because her name "SOUNDED" / appeared
Blackï¿½. we are talking about 'ethics'.  Even the
fact that we develop coded language and euphemisms
that are secretly used around business forums, like
- "Ooh!! I put Shantae under "File 13" - speaks
directly to the kind of ethics we employ during our
white employment.

Life, Liberty, and the Pursuit of happiness is a
noble construct; but how do you achieve that when
the rules are stacked against you?? When 'basic
opportunities' are denied to you?? Even
generationally speaking, as I have mentioned it
above, where ï¿½ somehow, despite all that has been
allowed or disavowed TO ANY ONE FAMILY -- you are
expected to thrive WITH NOTHING IN YOUR HAND!!  This
is the mythical saga that white people narrate when
they simply look at a Black person, and try to
devise and understand "why they are in the place
that they're in??" (with a scowl or a frown of
disgust upon their face). Somehow, white people
feelï¿½. "All is forgiven, the field is now levelï¿½
Sorry for the past faux pas, Black man!" - even
though, deep down inside, the residual affects of
their past twisted ethics are actively, the most
deadly undertow still silently sweeping people away.
People who don't measure up, Brown and Black people,
Immigrants and Foreigners, random sufferers outside
of nepotism, and those whose names or image does not
FIT the company mission statement. It's ridiculous!!
And people tremble at the idea of possibly thinking
to join certain professions, for fear of being
blackballed, black-walled, whitewashed, or
blackmailed for being Black in an all white working
environment. You may have heard recently (2018/19)
how that General Motors in Michigan had several
federal complaints filed on them for years of
repeated racially charged harassments against many
Black workers in the plants and in the corporate
offices, ï¿½.in 2019ï¿½. Really??!!!  These Black
PROFESSIONALS daily suffering racial degradation in
the name of poor business practices and unpurged
biased unethical standards.

So, the idea of "Business Ethics" actually, has not
yet touched the bottom of its own murky ocean floor.
And again, to ask the questionï¿½. "Where are you
located regarding this subject??" - you'll notice
how it starts to tighten that proverbial power tie
around your neck. Now, as the air is currently
flowingï¿½ Let's go back and visit our new Black
friend. When you think of someone who has chosen the
profession of being an Architectï¿½. How many white
architects do you know (personally)?? Can you name
them??  Now, asking the exact same question: How
many Black Architects do you know (personally)?? Can
you name them?? -- Now, let's ask about Doctorsï¿½
white and Black; How many do you know (personally)??
Can you name them?

Now, your new Black friendï¿½.. What does he do for
a living?? Does he work in the same building or
office as you??  [And, I strongly urgeï¿½ DO NOT ASK
THIS; that would be uncouth and against corporate
payroll policy]. Does your friend (especially if
he's in the same jobï¿½. ) make the same amount of
money as you??  You may want to assume to know the
answer to that question. Undoubtedly, as you get to
know him / her better, you may discover more about
them and their work-related encounters with racism.
At best, one can go to college, complete their
degree(s), hone in on their particular profession at
a particular company, and then work hard to thrive,
succeed, earn a promotion or two - and (hopefully)
never have to speak of those pauses, and periods of
incredible doubt as to whether they were doing
enough, are in the right place, or felt the need to
move on because of some power-tripping boss who
seeks their demise.  But, I will go on record here
as sayingï¿½. "That rarely happens!!"  In any case,
Black people are expected to be THE MOST ETHICAL of
any person standing in the room, yetï¿½. as is
displayed in movies, like - "Wolf of Wall Street"
and so, so, so, so, many others, the young white
brilliant power-mover ruthlessly fenagles his way to
the top / corner office.  More pointedlyï¿½. one of
my favorites (especially as I am NOT a fan of Ben
Affleck, especially after his Professor Gates
incident) is the 2002 Feature Film starring Samuel

L. Jackson -- "Changing Lanes"!!  The title is an
apt description of how - one bad moment in ethical
judgement spirals into a tornado of lives on the
verge of being needlessly and shamelessly destroyed.

In real life, even as in movies, we hold out these
double standards as badges of honor in white
America. The Rolex graciously given for the team's
most profitable agent. Standing next to his Black
co-worker who did EVERYTHING by the book, but white
boy Chad gets all the honor for being an amazing and
crafty liar. He's ambitious!! He's on FIRE!! Andï¿½
he hasn't gotten caught!!  This is the "NORM" that
is represented as ethics and desirable business
practices. As we pointed out before,
historicallyï¿½. There could be one person, who
feels he's keenly able to wield the sword of
achievement - and get away with murder, but it's
usually NOT just one person. That kind of mindset
thrives more productively in a group. Hence, the
now, multi-layered theme under the definably growing
title-umbrella of "Racism". There's no putting off
the lucrative bobbles and trinkets that are
purchased as childish rewards for ungodly wealth.
And, one never blinks at the idea that their
unethical behavior causes someone else to suffer.
Think about advertisement and marketing, how we
boldly target people, and their computers or phones
- to gain the upper-hand on how they will choose to
swipe their debt-ridden credit cards next.  And, if
it were not for many protests, inside and outside of
these companies offices and boardrooms - they would
shamelessly market cigarettes, drugs, and liquor
exclusively to the black community uninterrupted.
We are not seeing enough change, and many people
feel powerless to do anything about it. They yellï¿½
it's UNETHICAL!! And it is, we cannot afford the
time to launch a full scale boycott or legal court
hearing to change this undercurrent of forced
consumerism. It's a different form of slavery!! If
you have ever noticedï¿½. You will NOT find a
bookstore (like Barnes and Noble) or a Starbucks in
the heart *or surrounding areas of the Black
community. And, it's an accepted ethical practice,
so long as we are making money.  But if you turn

your head three ways, you'll find a check-cashing
store. It's no wonder Black people are quick to
pronounce someone a 'racist' or declare 'racism'.
We have learned times 10,000 - exactly what a racist
looks like, and what racism itself feels, sounds,
and looks like. And I'm not speaking in projections.

Over many years, from having dogs attack us in the
'50's, to desegregating schools and needing military
assistance to enter, to the current day police
brutality and rampant popular use of excessive force
by the police - we have developed a built-in radar,
that within seconds of hearing someone speak and/or
being pulled into an unforeseen situation, we know
emphatically what a racist looks like and are very
clear what racism is.  Consider at this point, the
above points that I've outlined for youï¿½.. Do you
believe that all Black people are completely blind
and oblivious to the philosophies and daily
practices of the white world - clearly operating in
favor of themselves??? That was a question. It is
NOT rhetorical. Every white person, especially those
suffering from white fragility, need to be able to
cognitively reach the self-appointed conclusion of
these truths. You do not want to continue to dismiss
the lie, nor dismiss the truth. The evolution that
is occurring during the reading of this book - is
supported by many other authors, but I insist on the
targeted healing of your heart, mind, body, soul,
and spirit. So, can we clear up every incidence of
corruption in businessï¿½.??? Probably not.  But the
hope isï¿½ that, if someone (in the future) calls
you a racist for speaking your mindï¿½ you PAUSE.
You pause and consider these pages, understanding
that they MAY NOT be speaking about something that
is overt, or even instigated by you!! They may just
be shining a spotlight on a treacherous situation,
that you yourself may unknowingly be involved inï¿½.
And it may be ruining someone's life, someone's
image, someone's chances to advance  or progress;
you may be unravelling something that represents
healing that was set in motions by that person's
family member, decades ago - or last week. You may
be RE-CREATING America's bloody history.

Dare I even sayï¿½. To all of these people who feel
it necessary to call the police on a Black person
(in your immediate vicinity) - just because the wind
blew! -- YOU, white person,ï¿½. who feels this
strange ethical pulse to assert your rights, is
absolutely NOT thinking that that same event could
mean DEATH to the innocent Black person involved in
your spider's web. It's NOT a balanced scale!!
[911] "How may I help you..?!!"  --  There's a
strange, big, scary black man standing about 10 feet
away from meï¿½. And I feel threatened for my life,
because when he glanced at meï¿½. the wind blew
really hard on me from his direction, and it knocked
my hat off. Can you send the police right away;
please ï¿½ HURRY!!"  Meanwhile, this poor Black man
is entangled in this black widow's web (of lies) -
ready to be eaten alive, and spit out like trash.

I'm sure business ethics can be taught. And I'm
2000% certain, they can be enforced. But one's moral
fiber is what's called into question, every single
time. That internal mechanism. Somewhere in their
subconscious mind (or the DNA that has been passed
down to them), they have this set of images that
emboldens them to proceed within business in a way
that's informs their ego - that, "it is okay"!!
Okay to kill, steal, lie, and then show up to church
on Sunday and not feel a pinch of guilt - because
they volunteer for their white community, or they
write a check in support of charities.

It may seem worthlessï¿½. But I completely HOLD that
it ï¿½is ï¿½.worthwhile - to try and settle some of
the discrepancies that arise as untested and
unchallenged ethical slights, by bringing them to
the law.


Building #3: Let's call it - The Department of Law!!
The first of these ethical slights (in my opinion)
are classic American staples and tenets like,
"INNOCENCE UNTIL proven guilty in a court of law";
"protect and serve"; and "with liberty and justice

for all".  I vehemently insert here, that NO police
officer should ever be allowed to remain on any
police force, nationwide, if they violate these
statutes by acting as the judge, the jury, and the
executioner against any American citizen, from today
moving forward.  And in those instances where it
seems that this might happenï¿½. We raise our voice
(white people included), we make a phone call (white
people included), we use our platform and bring
attention to the issue (white people included); am I
making my point clear?!? And I absolutely intend to
highlight and include "white people" as a group that
IS NOT SEPARATE from Black. My other reason to
target "WHITE PEOPLE" - is to make a future point,
understanding that, based on information from
Jacqueline Battalora PhD. J.D. -- white people (as a
titled group or race classification) did not exist
before 1681. We will touch more upon that point
later in this dept. Yet somehow, using exclusionary
tactics, disruptive and biased law enforcement, and
upholding poor judgement - we desecrate the values
we so readily claim to love. So as it is, for those
three small powerful statements (that supposedly
undergird our country) that you find people like
Colin Kaepernick, taking a knee during the National
Anthem, in protest to the above, during his
spotlight moments and in the most visible and
effective way - during what some might call, "his
job".  But, no one's job description should take
precedent above the effective operation of our
government and judicial system. He, just like one
statement I made above: "Why doesn't he shut up and
just move on already?!!" - has had that verbally and
non-verbally hurled at him by the billions, yetï¿½
his political expediency and subsequent silence
branded him in the golden light of EXACTLY what an
American is.  He, in the eyes of every Black
family, sacrificed himself on our behalf.  We (all)
couldn't afford to lose our jobs, we (all) could not
see ourselves as being as effective as he was. So we
applauded him, and we knelt when we couldï¿½ even in
private, in the covered protection and comfort of
our homes.  We [collectively] KNELT with him!!

Now to his antagonists, I said thisï¿½. Maybe some
of you will recognize it:  "ï¿½..We hold these
truths to be self-evident, that all men are created
equal, that they are endowed by their Creator with
certain unalienable Rights, that among these are
Life, Liberty and the pursuit of Happiness. -- That
whenever any Form of Government becomes destructive
of these ends, it is the Right of the People to
alter or abolish it, and to institute new
Government, laying its foundation ï¿½. To effect
their Safety and Happiness. ï¿½..But when a long
train of abuses and usurpations, pursuingï¿½., it is
their right, it is their duty, to throw off such
Government, and to provide new Guards for their
future security."

This is our Declaration of Independence. And, while
it speaks expressly of the time in which it was
written, we still hold these truths to be self-
evident. Shall we write a new one?? Should we start
over??  Somewhere, somehowï¿½. Even today, we want
to make all of the aforementioned words, ANNULLED!!
We quickly want to make Colin K. wrong for doing
what this holy document declares.  He was more
American than us allï¿½. He was even MORE American
then his antagonists.  They (mostly white people)
GOT IT VERY WRONG!!  Black people would call them
[collectively], Racists - you understand why?

You cannot place saluting a flag OVER a person's
life, and safety.
You cannot place a song OVER a police officer's duty
to exercise proper judgement.
You cannot place a football game OVER someone's
RIGHT to live.
You cannot place this country's negative history
OVER a man's expression to protest that negative
history.
All of these things are saying the same thing as the
"Declaration" above them. It is his / our
unalienable Right.

Not that there's an excitement to calling a
collection of people, racist. It's more the exercise
of a muscle; a knee-jerk. And, of courseï¿½ this is

NOT to make an excuse. If it is ever expressed at all, it might show up in a conversation. So, does the law support our declaration?? Emphaticallyï¿½ NO!! It would seem that it tries everything to do the reverse!

Law is supposed to be impartial and unbiased. We can use the "Declaration of Independence" and, in a flash, use our time machine to transport ourselves back in time - and see the crafters sitting, trying to determineï¿½ HOW are we going to ENFORCE these governmental ideas?? So, they designed a judicial system; From judges and courts, all the way down to police officers, and the very democratic idea of "safety" to the country as a whole. Lawmakers keeping the people and the process in mind, came up with the checks and balances that we enlist today. BUTï¿½ Do we really believe that our judicial system has withstood the ills of racism?? I can quickly contest that, there are not many things that can withstand racism! Under the concept of "upholding the law" - opinions start to fly. People feel passionate, empowered, and ultimately have an idealists' view - about WHAT WORKS!!

To find out what works, you would both look to the people and to the processï¿½. The people who contest, might say: "The Law is broken!!" and they should be heard!! But sadlyï¿½. And I'll allow this to be one of my main and final points for this Department is: Racism would seek to ignore or silence those people BECAUSE you (as a white man or an avid supporter of the law across all racial lines) FEELS that the law [works just fine] FOR YOU and that those others are wrong, or that they are stupid.ï¿½. I'm using "the word" RACISM here becauseï¿½ I honestly feel that it can have BOTH a negative and a positive connotation. And, I will use a few generalizations as well - to try and further clarify my bilateral point.

Positively speakingï¿½. Racism - that is used against another - provides an opportunity "to hear" and "to learn" where things have gotten off-track. Negatively speakingï¿½. Racism - someone is always

going to feel attacked, or is going to want to
ignore what [actually] is being said, but, it's
coming across in a more "coded" manner.  And where
emotions are skewed  - things are never clearly
understood by anyone or all.  Soooooï¿½ï¿½ let's
quickly look at how racism might be influencing
these twisted connotations of proper law.

As a group, within the prism of racism (and using
sweeping generalizations), white people
unconsciously feel that Black people are stupid, or
[if speaking code:] do not have the capacity or
desire to UPHOLD the law; we are inferior and 'could
never understand the law'. They (white people) tend
to exclude everyone based upon a bad personal
experience or something they saw on the news. In
fact, Black people - truthfully - do not trust the
law, and are overall consider to be a violent people
because we (seemingly) "RESIST" - when [if speaking
code:] we are just tired of ill treatment and are
fearful of our lives.  And isn't it amazing how BOTH
GROUPS, white / Blackï¿½. Policemen / Civilianï¿½.
Feel like they are in fear (of losing) their
life??!! Wow.  And, sadly it is NOT a common thought
thatï¿½ Officers (not to point them out, but just
making a point) are the ones with all the government
"authority" (so to speak). They should be able to
see their roles as an active, living, and alive
portrayal of what the forefathers intended when they
spoke the word: SAFETY.  Insteadï¿½. They do the
opposite. Nowï¿½. While I am speaking in
generalizations, you can swing to the other side of
the same spectrum - where you typically will find a
white person trying to use the law in their favor,
or using the law as their own personal Billy-club.
They never want to appear violent, so they hide
their hands while issuing secret jabs - in the name
of justice. So, (again using sweeping
generalizations), most Black people can expect most
white people to "manipulate the law" for their OWN
benefit, or try to lean so heavily ON IT - in the
form of patriotism - that they horde those benefits
against anyone else who does not fit within their
extremely narrow, mentally twisted, judicial
blinders.  They literally - TRY - to take the law

into their own hands, as one 'having the right' to
it. Hence, our second amendment rights arguments in
this country.  BUT NO ONE - EVER - stops to see -
how can we better secure what our forefathers and
lawmakers purposed - to uphold the ENTIRE country,
without contrived, white western, maverick-like
biases??

It sounds IDEAL even to say it or write it on the
page.... yet, it's the very theme behind a lot of
evil and corrupt people, even religious people
(namely "Evangelicals") who prophesy that this
president, Donald J. Trump - somehow brilliantly and
valiantly upholds all of these AMERICAN TENETS
(simply because he is rich and white). But here, I'd
like to add more of what I mentioned above. We are
grateful for such people as Nina Jablonski PhD. -
The Evan Pugh Professor of Anthropology at
Pennsylvania State University and the
aforementioned, Jacqueline Battalora PhD. J.D.
(specifically) who asserted... and I quote:  --
"white people did not exist before 1681." She also
states that "White supremacy has been embedded in
the United States of America from its founding as a
matter of law".  In the 1600 Colonial America, Pre-
"Bacon's Rebellion", a law was passed in 1664
regarding "British and other freeborn women who
marry enslaved negro men" (or men of African
descent) - would be punished. Now, enter the
secretly famous Antimiscegenation law, prohibiting
mixed marriages [here] - which was one of the first
places to specifically and insidiously announce the
term "white people" in order to destructively
alienate and further distinguish between persons of
color, People of African descent, Native Americans,
and other non-white people... to enlist an inferior
tone, and create verbiage that could be 'legalized'.
This law lasted for 300 years! It was declared
'unconstitutional' in 1967 -- in THIS 20th Century
lifetime -- after the ruling of "Loving vs.
Virginia". It was a North American term derived from
the 'British Common Law' of its time. Hence, the
1861 interpretation reads: "British and other [white
women]" thus made it illegal to marry an enslaved
negro or person of African descent. This punishment

was for the landowners who encouraged mixed marriage
- to build their assets, their labor-force, and
sought to own another human being as chattel or
property; and of course, punished the female causing
her to lose her rights, and began some of the
initial punishing practices to come later - denying
Black people the right to hold a public office,
denying Black people the right to own a gun, or (in
some cases) own property, or denying Black people
the right to testify against white people in a court
of law.  To further bring this point to a current-
day recognizable light.... Imagine, you as a Black
man cannot own a gun, but your slavemaster (or now
freed white indentured slave) receives a gift and is
paid a gun and gun powder = [while] The Black freed
slave gets nothing; so, who is protected from
whom.... and who has lost power to defend his
family?? Sounds eerily similar to authorities
reliving their twisted and corrupt DNA from past
generations in the form of police brutality and the
ridiculous and senseless shooting of unarmed Black
men and women. Imagine, it's against the law to
marry a white person.... thus we run headlong into
the story of Emmitt Till = killed for looking at a
white woman or the Central Park Five accused of a
crime they did not commit or as I joked from line #1
of this book... Some random white person calling the
police on a Black person, or Trayvon Martin's killer
- George Zimmerman acting in a position of authority
that was not his to claim, or the crazy white man
who shot a Black man outside of a convenience store
(in Florida) when he was SHOVED for very rudely
speaking to the Black man's partner who was
temporarily parked in a handicap space... another
Black man shot dead in front of his Black son and
wife in 2018. And lastly... Imagine the boom of
white lives that are born from these back-water
laws. All claiming and identifying with the word /
term: WHITE -- as if given a card to a secret order
filled with privilege and inherent superiority. A
title that was never legally accepted!!  But, what
was implied, as Battalora stated - is a socio-
economic division and divide between whites (as
ALWAYS above) and Blacks as well as other Non-wites
(as ALWAYS below). Obviously... that ideology still

exists and is running rampant today. The message to
white people is very engrained and very clear!! In
fact, Battalora states that there was a
Naturalization Law - which stated... You had to be a
white person... to become a citizen of the newly
formed United States of America in 1790, and was
considered VALID all the way thru 1952 - when that
was finally ruled out.

It's no wonder that people of color feel this
country has been built on our back, our blood,
sweat, and tearsï¿½ In not one of the aforementioned
Departments can we get a fair shake. And, as I move
forwardï¿½ you'll be reminded that this "white man's
silver thread" was woven into an already established
fabric, and hidden there ingeniously by those who
sought to CONTROL someone else.  Investigating white
fragility as it relates to "control" - basically,
solely, wants to "control" whether the entire
conversation is had or not. So, you may feel like -
"None of this applies to me!!" and on the surface,
there might be a tiny bit of truth to that.  So,
very careful personal investigation and self-
examination of the lawï¿½. Even how you may feel
it's being used FOR YOU (in your favor) or against
you, is CRITICAL.

On this fictitious university campus, white
fragility quietly shunning the sun's knowledgeable
rays, still hopes to stand (self-righteously) as a
beautiful fragrant flower for all to see - hoping to
blend into the landscape while trickily avoiding the
student gatherings. White fragility secretly
scoffing at all the others who sincerely participate
to gain this higher education, because
intellectually speaking... they don't have the time
to EXHAUST, cannot see clear to winning the
argument, or simply refuse to place value or
importance on an experience that is so far outside
of themselves... They stamp it as - "a waste". It is
the very dung that fertilizes them.... and they feel
comfortable in its nutrients.  Though the campus is
providing a power-house of protection, they act as
if their feet are cemented or weighed down. And
subconsciously here, it may be a family member's

bigoted reminder cropping up from days and decades
gone by. However, if we are forging ahead... to
assist those who may be stuck in their white
fragility deadzone (to give you an action you can
control): ...WHAT CAN HAPPEN NEXT IN THE REAL
WORLDï¿½. After finding your new black friend, our
next endeavor will beï¿½ finding a Black-owned
business to support, or maybe hosting a dinner party
for some people who don't look like you. This may
not be something that you can magically entertain in
one day; you may need to plan.  But, as alwaysï¿½ BE
UPFRONT!! And, I'll place a small footnote here to
be discussed later; NO TAPPING OUT!!!

Confronting your invisible ignorance will only come
to light in the close, and personal confines of an
evening spent at a dinner table, or living room
loungeï¿½ laughing and talking about who we really
areï¿½ and where we come from. Do you have brothers
or sisters?? Did you go to college?? What's the
dream that you have in your heart and mind that you
have yet to achieve?? What dreams HAVE YOU achieved,
that you're proud of??  Listening to stories,
visiting neighborhoods that you ordinarily would
not, or realizing that there are places of business
hard at work - trying to stay afloat and/or thrive.
This is what will be "your reason".  When you start
to learn and hear these various stories that others
[Black people] deem important to themselvesï¿½. You
expand, you grow, you graduate a small portion of
yourself and let go of the smallest fragment of that
white fragility - acting as a monster in your mind.
You gain - invaluable education. Which leads us to
our next Department.

Building #4: Let's call it - The Department of
Education!!
You may notice that some of these Department
descriptions will get shorter, but NONE has more
immediate depth than the Department of Education.
For example, those obvious historical points like
the segregated schools of the '50's will shrink in
comparison to the constantly unravelling knowledge
of countless human lives who's stories will never be
told. People who died, hanging from a tree. People

who were beaten with baseball bats or policeman's
batons (just for being Black, and not for being
criminals). People who were shot with guns, or
dragged behind trucks because they said, Hello, or
merely looked at a white person. In fact, you could
talk to 100 Black people, and each one of them can
tell you a tragic story from their family's past (or
one from his/her very own life). And, it is of the
utmost importance that you BELIEVE and listen, and
feel / empathize with what they are telling you.  It
may even be cathartic - for them to divulge these
experiences and may serve as a pivotal (positive or
negative) subconscious moment.

Personal stories not only provide an opening, but in
the 'human quotient' brings us all to a point that
is basically unarguable. As humans, we all go
through painsï¿½. We all have stories to tell;
definable stories. They provide a great source of
education and insight, thus they should be received
as such. Here's a story and a not-so-amusing-
anecdote or two from my own personal life regarding
both my Grandmother and Grandfather. Here it is:


MY GRANDPARENTS EDUCATION


Both of my grandparents only had elementary school
level educations because they had to work, could not
go to school in their area of the deep South, or
some other reason that they never acknowledged,
spoke about, or felt the need to share in light of
their current day life situations. In fact,
(especially older) African-Americans are not
typically known for speaking about hardships that
they've had to live thruï¿½. Yet another HUGE reason
to listen when someone is sharing from their past. I
could tell even when Grandma sent me to the store
that her handwriting and spelling was "questionably
shaky". But, againï¿½ it was NOT ever something that
a Black child would launch as an interrogation
against your elder; it was strictly off-bounds and
completely out of the question and represented a

form of deep, deep disrespect to pry. But, from what
I understood or heardï¿½ my Grandmother had about an
8th or 9th grade education. And, my grandfather had
about a 6th grade education. Although, despite his
limited schooling, my Grandpa was a business owner
of a Billiard hall, with approx. 10 rentable
sleeping quarters above. As a child, my brother and
I used to go there and play atop the pool tables -
when the place was closed and my grandparents were
cleaning the place from top to bottom. My brother
and I would roll the balls back and forth, drink
Coca Cola out of the old-school bottle machine -
where you open the door and pull the paid bottle
out. We always would get a few pieces of candy like
Baby Ruth's, or Almond Joy'sï¿½ and we never took
too much, because we also knew where all this candy
came from, when Grandpa would take us with him to
the Wholesalers warehouse - to buy what was needed
to make a profit. This is one small memory that
shaped me and my entrepreneurial spirit that still
thrives inside of me to this day.  Their lack of
education (though) did not stop them from loving us,
loving meï¿½. They were as amazing as Grandma's
homemade jelly. There house filled with structure,
and routine, and patience, and unspoken love. They
found other ways to express thatï¿½ one of which
was, making sure that I never ever went hungry, or
felt unsafe.

As for people of their time, they were blessed
enough to move North, and even took the risk of
owning a business where other's merely looked for
work to sustain their families. My Grandfather had
two children with my Grandmother - who already had 5
children from her previously deceased husband and
their marriage. My Grandmother was a housewife, so
this was not today's double income earning
household.  The several years gap in the children's
ages probably helped a lotï¿½ as their home, the
only one I know, had two bedrooms, and a sealable
den downstairs that served as the master bedroom off
of the kitchen. The other children were closer to
adulthood, and in a few cases, were starting their
own families - where my mother's nieces and nephews
were older than her; they grew up together - as

peers. We were the Black Brady Bunch, and it was not
strange, nor did we require special titles for each
other. The family (children) respected my
grandfather as their grandfatherï¿½ and everyone was
happy. So, when I think of the multitudes of other
Black families that struggled, weren't business
owners, may have been split, may have been stunted
due to similar poor educational backgroundsï¿½
obviously, they will not be the same - so I'm
extremely grateful. Not every Black family has been
able to get past slavery, racism, and other horrible
events with white people who meant them no good. It
is literally, the luck of the draw!!

The 2nd story of my Grandfather was a shock, if not
outright scary. I was about 7 or 8 years old. It was
not common or regular that we made a trip 'down
south' to the states where my grandparents were born
and raised; Georgia, for her, and Alabama, for him.
On this tripï¿½. We were going to see his family /
sisters.  As we are driving in whatever state - I'm
sure we were at least south of Tennessee or Virginia
- perhaps South Carolinaï¿½. While driving at a
regular speed limit, basically enjoying the ride
with my Mom in the front seat, my Grandfather
driving, my Grandmother, my brother, and I in the
back seatï¿½.. our joy was interrupted. Out of
nowhere, police sirens, a cop pulled us overï¿½ and
even at 7 years old, I knew he wasn't speeding!! And
so, he calmly pulled over with a small grunt. And
the next thing that happenedï¿½. has never happened
before or since in knowing my G'pa's temperament.
He stopped the car and QUICKLY turned around and
spoke to everyone sayingï¿½ "Don't NOBODY say
NOTHIN'!! ï¿½. Just be quiet; do you hear me?!!" -
with this SHARP look in his eyes and TONE in his
voiceï¿½. and, I felt like a vault that was slammed
shut!!  He turned back around, and next, the officer
slowly walked up to the driver side window.

Rolling down the window, the policeman asked for the
driver's license and registration, and my
Grandfather said, "Yes Sir!!". I could tell the
immediate disposition and posture of my G'pa was
different as the policeman then questioned, "How

fast do you think you were going, BOYï¿½ where you all going?!!" (I thoughtï¿½ "BOY???") - and my early 50's year old Grandfather almost whispering answered the question. My Grandfather, who was a very broad, 6 foot 3 inch tall man, with a caramel complexion, and a rough reputation from his pool hall persona ï¿½ seemed to almost be groveling as this policeman further mouth-off to my still and quiet Grandfather (calling him a 'boy' at least two more times that I can recall). With a head nod, "yes sir, yes sir", and the traffic warning that was given upon his return, no ticket written, and the policeman handing him back his infoï¿½ we slowly pulled away to continue our journey. Thankfullyï¿½. Nothin else happened, and in comparison to similar stories we hear todayï¿½ this one might even seem mild.  But understandï¿½. My G'pa was like a superhero in my eyes, and to see someone disrespecting him (in front of us / me) left this "impression of disrespect" (by an officer) indelibly printed on my mind. An encounter, thankfully, I've never had to go through with my own father.  Yet, as I've statedï¿½ NEVER BEFORE had I seen my G'pa speak so defiantly and fearfully LIKE THAT in my whole entire time on earth with him.  He was quietly sweet and loving to his grandchildren. Yet, in that unnecessarily rude moment, he understood - in a flash - where we were; what the climate wasï¿½ and how it could get out of hand. I cannot imagine the underlying fear that may have gripped him to imagine what would be necessary to protect his family should things go wrong.  I don't know if he carried a gun in his carï¿½ but I know he could shoot one, and owned a rifle that sat in the corner behind a vanity or tall chest of drawers (whichever was decoratively placed in the ONE corner). No one EVER, ever touched it. It was concealed in a beautiful deer-hide colored, suede and leather case, that form the shape of a gunï¿½ so, there was not much confusion as to what it was. And, although I can describe the case, we were absolutely forbidden to ask, look at, or touch it. On that road though, if G'pa had a weapon, I can applaud him just for being calm because even in my mindï¿½. It looked like it was very difficult.

The police officer's demeanor was an education that
day tooï¿½ I also recall his stature, his face, and
his attitude and words towards my Grandfather. He
was NOT NICE - at all. He only addressed my
Grandfather and did not acknowledge anyone else in
the car. I recall he kept one hand on his gun - both
hands appeared to be on his hips. I don't know if
the holster was unclipped (I was too young to know
about or notice that), and I didn't know what he was
stopping us for other than his questions. And soï¿½.
As a result of these and history - Black people
almost refuse to trust the police.

Education by books, education by life experience,
education by examples and theories all serve
various ends, that are not ever the same. Yet, it's
something that everyone needs - and the branches,
however supportive, are extremely long, and extend
very, very far in all directions. They are the re-
livable pages of the books that we read; hence our
next building.

Building #5: Let's call it - The Department of
History!!
The Department of History is the one place where
white people could easily say, "I'll start here"ï¿½
but upon entry, begin to cringe because they
realize, all those redacted pages and lost volumes
are very much intact in THIS library.  Instead of
trying to [accept] what's here, what's realï¿½..
and, as is particularly obvious with white
fragility, white people try to avoid the harshness
of history.  This building draws a lot of attention
and looks attractive to those walking onto the
campus of racism for the first time. It is the
school / department that undergoes the most change
in its structure on the campusï¿½. because people
like to come here and tear down, rebuild, tear down,
rebuild, and ultimately, tear down - but never
completely. I think, that they think that they can
tear it down for goodï¿½. when all they're really
doing is prepping the ground for a more elaborate
look and design. The content is never in jeopardy,
and the treasured items are never lost, although,
with every changeï¿½ there seems to be more

discovered, unknown, valuable, historical
information to add to its collection. So, though it
looks possible, and we prefer to not waste
materials, an audacious white person who dreams of
the obliteration of this build - does not actually
accomplish this, nor could ever rid themselves of
its penetrating sting

The souls speak louder and louder, and the changes,
mistakes, and omissions become glaringly clearer -
as if someone opened a fresh can of truth, getting
rid of the ominous odor of lies passed down through
the centuries to either, make one look wiser, or
make another look ignorant. The fact that someone
feels the need to erase history and in essence,
erase the voices of the souls who reside within
history - have NOT heard them, have not learned from
them, and are NOT listening. What does history
represent?? Well, what it should (ideally) represent
are our proudest moments and achievements, such as
when the country was founded. But, usually, we pick
names, characters, and events that carry a theme or
an idea - even if the theme or idea is unjust and
evil.  But... let me give a prophetic newsflash
right here: The Future foundations regarding racism
and the like require all apparent truth.

I don't think that anyone will necessarily argue
that - TRUTH should be apparent to all. Truth should
not and (futuristically speaking) WILL NOT be
relegated to 'the few'. Even as I quickly denote
some things in these upcoming Departments - you can
immediately see the differences that will be
expected and conversely, will not be tolerated ever
again. Allow me a few liberties to elaborate.


Building #6: Let's call it - The Department of
Medicine
Experiments done on black people - and the White
ideal of being a "Good, moral person" in the face of
atrocities fabricated in the name of medicine and
otherwise (the hypocratic oath hoax).

Building #7: Let's call it - The Department of
Entertainment
The separation of Rock and Roll, Music stolen, the
issue of cultural appropriation, today's black
filmmakers = and Hollywood's debate whether they are
"bankable"

Building #8: Let's call it - The Department of Real
Estate
Red lining, other housing discrimination, land that
was never yours to take, 40 acres and a mule

Building #9: Let's call it - The Department of
Agriculture and innovation
Inventions created by people of color, free labor of
the former slave days, the return to community
gardens in the urban food deserts

Building #10: Let's call it - The Department of
Communication
media who raises double standards: thugs (black) vs.
passionate crowd of protestors (white) - "Fine
people on both sides", body cams, CNN vs. Fox News,
why "TAPPING OUT" is the new hero of racism


WHAT IS "TAPPING OUT"


This might be the easiest paragraph in the whole
book.... but please understand, its criminality
reaches into other realms - as it represents a
person, who, for example learning about white
fragility - could be seen as intentionally killing a
teachable moment, or a friendship, etc. It is very
situational, and requires a surgeons skilled hand.
Tapping out is exactly as it sounds. Think of a
wrestling match, where the opponent is
unquestionably pinned to the ground... and in PAIN.
How long is he going to stay in the fight?? How much
is too much?? Will he pound "tap" the mat to signify
to the referee that he is out; he is done... He
quits!! To make it Biblical for a moment.... when
Jesus was about to be betrayed... "HE TOLD THE

DISCIPLES BEFORE-HAND" that it would happen, but no
one believed him, and they all professed, "No
Master... we love you... we will follow your lead!!"
But, hence... we know Judas, the very next day,
betrayed Him with a kiss for a bag of silver.  Now,
imagine your new black friend is in a situation, and
you are asked to be his witness. You've been with
him the whole time... but, you don't want to get
your hands dirty (so-to-speak), and you don't want
to be involved!! Congratulations, Mr. / Mrs. White
Fragility!! You have just betrayed your Black
friend!! You did not "have his 6" - as the military
might say in the thick of war.  It is literally,
that serious, to a person of color, befriending a
white person, who knows the truth.... but won't
speak up or act on that truth. Mind you, it does not
matter if that situation is great or small.... and
it's not a license to say, "I told you so" to your
white friend, or to say,"I knew you were NO good!" -
but, it more closely represents THE EXACT MOMENT
when you should be able to see with crystal clear
definition - the TRUTH - in the moment, as a Black
person might perceive it.  In fact, you should be
able to see it [the injustice committed] without
prompting or assistance.  If your friend is an
alcoholic... you don't leave him at the bar... nor
do you take him to the bar to further screw up his
life. The keyword here is: "INTENTIONAL".  Why is
this a big deal??  Simply put: two voices are better
than one. There is such a thing as - One white
person will easily and quickly believe another white
person.... and thus, we have two people who have
been exposed to the truth (or "a truth") and
hopefully experiences an enlightening (subconscious)
flare. And you start to understand the importance of
standing in another man's shoes... you start to
appreciate his journey more and better.  So a quick
recap:
1)   . You never give up on your friend.
2)   . You never  give up on the truth.
3)   . You always speak out - no matter what - as one
     who has been given insight (by way of
     connection, knowledge, etc)
4)   . You demonstrate "love" by way of understanding
     - standing in another man's shoes; secure and

respect your friend's cultural differences and
perspectives as good and worthy of protection -
as if it were [YOU] yourself.

As someone who has now taken the tour of our campus
of racism... you should be finding yourself in race
discussions more often (and potentially, more
easily), and whether or not it's with a Black
person, or other persons of color, you never "tap
out" of the discussion. STAY IN IT... you are in the
mode of listening, feeling, and learning. Be overly
willing to listen and not respond to every point
with argument. The same is true... ACTUALLY, even
more so... if you have the light of insight on your
side, and, if you are speaking with a white
person... speaking about race or racism in general;
you never "tap out"!! You now, must demonstrate to
and for that white person, your passion for your
understanding of Black culture (as you know and
understand it). If you cannot do that
(effectively)... you have just learned your next
area of study, You now see the chink in your
'appreciation of black armour'. White fragility will
start to look like an excuse, because you realize...
that with assistance, none of this is IMPOSSIBLE!!
Your friend's brown or black skin IS NOT going
away... it is a color that can be appreciated like a
crayon in a box. You see what they see. You feel
what they might feel... and out of concern (even in
the moment, you can inquire about his/her
(psychological / emotional) health in the face of
injustice. You start to appreciate your own heritage
as a human being... now knowing, you came from that
person - you cannot love what you hate... human!!
So, use the campus wisely!!


WHAT EXACTLY IS WHITE FRAGILITY - DEFINED


So, although to some small degree, I think we all
know - what we believe - white fragility means. Of
course, I still want to delve into the subject more
deeply. I even decided to 'Google' the term and

definition of white fragility, just to see what
would come up!! Below is the actual definition that
appeared at the top of the screen.

white fragility
[white fragility]
NOUN
discomfort and defensiveness on the part of a white
person when confronted by information about racial
inequality and injustice.
"her indignant reaction comes off as the
quintessential combination of white fragility and
white privilege"

From
<https://www.bing.com/search?q=definition+of+white+f
ragility&form=EDNTHT&mkt=en-
us&httpsmsn=1&plvar=0&refig=007031de9405491afc5935cd
89feed74&sp=1&ghc=1&qs=SC&pq=definition+of+white+fa&
sc=8-
22&cvid=007031de9405491afc5935cd89feed74&cc=US&setla
ng=en-US>


This is a subject that is getting and gaining a lot
of interest in the media, the literary world, and is
on the hearts and minds of a lot of people.
Especially if those people want to know how to have
a better relationship or connections to "Black
Issues". Injustices in our world, and other things
that [truly] matter. I am excited to breach the
subject and avidly applaud those people are seeking
an active healing balm - whether for themselves or
someone they know or for those they don't know, but
choose to see, hear, and appreciate as it relates to
another's cultural experiences.

I have to be honestï¿½. I have not read any other
books (yet), nor have I had the need to steal
someone else's theories. In time, I'm sure that I
will cross paths with Dr. Robin DiAngelo (the only
name I've heard spoken / mentioned in relationship
to this subject). I'm sure there are others, and I
look forward to meeting them all - and maybe
discussing how this time of healing appears to them.
Certainly, all voices are needed where injustice is

found -- and I'm so thankful for those white voices
whose names I HAVE become accustomed to. People like
Tim Wise, and the amazing trailblazer, Jane Elliott
- who upon learning of Dr. Martin Luther King's
assassination, transformed her classroom into what
is now known as the "Brown eye / Blue eye
Experiment". They have taken a stanceï¿½ and I
believe there are others on the way.

 At first, to hear the term, "white fragility"
 (which may have even started as a social media
 meme), it may have sounded funny to its reader -
 like it did to me. I thought, "Do white people need
 a term to try to understand why they do or don't
 feel a certain kind of wayï¿½. as it relates to
 race or people other than themselves?!!?" And, I
 can say my laughter was a tiny bit knee-jerk. But,
 since I'm not the kind of person to laugh at other
 peoples' painï¿½. Whatever was felt at the point of
 seeing this new term aired, my thoughts with
 further research saidï¿½. "Okay, I can see it is
 necessary (and/or confusing as a whole to talk
 about it, intelligently). This pause absolutely DID
 NOT spark my need to sit down and write this book.
 But, as I do feel - time is of the essenceï¿½. I am
 immensely glad that you chose and are choosing to
 peruse its pages. What I felt most genuinely, was
 the need to talk about white fragility - from both
 perspectives: white and Blackï¿½ the subtleties
 therein and also ways to incorporate the active
 usage of our minds on this racial subject = as
 you've seen me already beginning to highlight in
 the previous pages and sections.

As a Highlight of contention: There are (sometimes)
a segment of people who will brandish unfiltered
words to refer to our collective group of people as,
"The BLACKS" -- which, I must tell you makes me want
to pull my hair out. I say that becauseï¿½ even the
tiniest omission, or seemingly unimportant (and
often unacknowledged) objectification turns into a
problem, like when you are talking about ï¿½."those
people". Well, I askï¿½ "Who are "THOSE PEOPLE" that
you are talking about.??!!! ï¿½. OHHhhhh, you
mean,ï¿½. "Black PEOPLE"??!!!  Even though you are

saying the word: BLACKSï¿½. It seems to be missing
some compassion, some dignity, and maybe some
obvious, overt respect.  I can almost hear someone
yellingï¿½ "Semantics!!" - but it's not.

To objectify someoneï¿½. As if you were saying,
"THOSE DAMN DOGS keep digging into my trash!!" You
can seem justified. But, when you are talking about
peopleï¿½. You USE the word, "people".  And soï¿½.
Separating out these differences early are
paramount.  Furthermore, it just doesn't sound right
- as well as being grammatically wrong:  EXAMPLE:
"[The Blacks] that I talk to are so mannerable, ï¿½
Oopps!! I mean. manageable, ï¿½Oopps!! What I mean
to say is, well-mannered. Awww, you know what I'm
trying to sayï¿½ï¿½!!!"

No!! ï¿½.We do NOT know what the hell you are trying
to say!!  ï¿½"Black people" need your clarity.

Just likeï¿½ It's not enough to sayï¿½. "You
shouldn't be racistï¿½ stop it!!" It's not even
enough to call someone a racist - when the person
merits it. But, what mechanisms can we use to really
affect change; good healthy change!! No doubt, no
one wants to be called a 'racist', but yet and
still, they areï¿½. Or they have "tendencies"
towards it. Today's political climate is like a
high harvest-time of fruit bearing trees with low
hanging "racially ripe" fruits.  And sadly, we need
not look very far to locate them. We can look
directly, repeatedly, immediately, and daily to our
esteemed White House, and to the man who occupies
it. In March 2019, President Donald Trump was
reported on social media and in news outlets to have
8000+ lies and gaffes since he's been in office.
And, as if we have all lost our minds, can pull up
several videos to support what we "THINK" we saw or
heard. He's the presidentï¿½. So, unless inertia
moves suddenly in a different direction -- He's HERE
already!! We have to deal with him and what comes
during his administration.

So, since I brought up Trumpï¿½. I would be remiss
in my duties if I did not also bring the actresses

Lori Loughlin and Felicity Huffman to the discussion
- who also alongside Donald Trump lied as reported
in March 2019, but we will discuss that prestigious
college admission bribe a little later. White
privilege aids the existence of White fragility.
And, I do think its unfair to always think that the
two are the same or similar.

BUTï¿½. I ask your apology (only for a second),
because - of course, I am not making this book about
politics, per se.
In my private world, my unimportant political
affiliations shows up several places after the
titles: Human, Male, Black, and God-fearing. I do
believe it is very important, however, when you are
getting to know a person, that you get to figure out
their layers.  And, as I go forward to discuss many,
many, many other thingsï¿½ you'll recall that I said
this pretty early on!!  I always start from the
position of "HUMAN" [first], but even as you already
know thisï¿½. You'll be able to say, "you know this
or that about me" - what do I mean??

You can deduce that I am NOT a Trump supporter!!
Beyond that point, I will take my place as the
SPOKESPERSON FOR ALL BLACK PEOPLE. I say that almost
jokingly becauseï¿½.. I know to very large
percentages, "Black people do not like, believe, or
support Pres. Donald Trump!!"  There I said itï¿½.
HA.  Yet, at various points, the President wants you
to believe that we do like himï¿½. We do support
himï¿½. We are so grateful [based upon his inflated
opinion and manipulated statistical numbers] that he
"gave us" better employment.  Most Black people
reading this book will be doubled over in laughter
right hereï¿½ for soooooooo many reasons!!

But, the main reason I want to present for these
above statements areï¿½.. We know a 'racist' when we
see one!!
President Donald Trump, who I actually really liked
as a reallly starï¿½ is so ill-equipped, and
furthermore, elitist - there's absolutely no way he
can relate to any Black person's 'Urban Plight'.
His background and his money places him in a

position to always keep his blinders on. He may not
even intentionally do thatï¿½. But he is
intentionally 'doing' just that because of his
position, and his psychological make-up; things that
he has been practicing for years and years and
years. If I can also quickly point out, at the time
that I am writing this bookï¿½. There's a movie
being made about the now [oxymoronic] infamously
innocent: "Central Park Five" ï¿½. Who at the height
of this past event was found publicly guilty by our
very own, President Donald J. Trump. He, finding
them guilty, in his court of public law, took it
upon himself to post a FULL PAGE AD in a New York
Newspaper - calling for the execution of these
[then] innocent teenagers. That's just one incident
to note; maybe I'll add another later.

So, when it comes to racist rants, where innocent
until proven guilty in a court of law, is deemed
unnecessaryï¿½. We, Black people, cringe and our
skin begins to crawl, boil, go numb!! It may not
even be the specific person themselvesï¿½ because,
until very recentlyï¿½ many people and people of
color, may not have known as much as they know right
now about our dear president. "Is it possible he
could still do a good job??!!..... SURE!!" - but,
"at whose expense?" ï¿½is the next logical question.
He, for me, in this book kind of represents an icon.
He's a paradigm!! He is a living breathing
representation of many white men in America - who
feel it's perfectly normal and right to be a racist.
They may not want to hear you call them that
wordï¿½. But, deep in their hearts, they know
emphatically that they are.  They HATE Black
peopleï¿½. And they want us all to die.

Now, there are variants to this. Some people just
don't want Black people in their neighborhood, or
dating their daughter. They don't want anyone TO
DIE.  There not as bad as the other guy, right??
WRONG!!  They are equally as bad. So, as we touch
upon white fragility, the definition of white
fragility, and the possible implications of white
fragility, regardless of where you fall on the 'HATE
Spectrum' (I just made that upï¿½.) we will examine,

in-depth, how well you are or ARE NOT wearing this
new label. We will try to consider all emotions as
valid. We will be empathetic - even while we are
pointing out 'the flaws'.  It is sincerely my belief
that this conversation and this subject matter are
decades past due for the center stage and the
spotlight.  Today, White fragility is ready for a
nice, golden, sun-drenched TAN.

Given the fact that this topic is so raw, and many
white peopleï¿½. even at a mere mention, flee. We
want you to know that we understand the angst that
comes with this stress-inducing verbiage. Butï¿½. I
usually liken this stress to one who is going to the
gym - to workout.  You've paid the membership by
having the book in your handsï¿½ and now, it's time
to honor the commitment you've set for yourself.
So, you jump in your car, and you drive yourself to
your swankiest gymï¿½ the one where all the cute
guys and girls go. You know, the one where you know
you'll be seenï¿½ and see a few beautiful bawdy
bodies that will challenge your soon-to-be, new and
improved you!! It's your first dayï¿½. And, you are
pretty geeked that you've made it this far - to
actually get in the car and goï¿½. Sooooo, applause
to you!!

Now, your first time at the gym, you look around,
and you sayï¿½"Hmmm?? Maybe I'll do the treadmill
first?!!"  Wise choice, becauseï¿½. YOU ARE SLOWLY
WORKING INTO THIS. To further elaborate, you are
taking the pressure off of yourself to look perfect
by next weekï¿½. THAT, in and of itself, is
encouragement. Butï¿½. Let's say one year has gone
by at this point hereï¿½. One year of being
committed to shaping down, and toning up. You stand
in the mirror and you actually see muscles!!
ï¿½.WOW!!  That's what this book and clearly
understanding this topic will do for you!
Absolutelyï¿½. Absolutely NO ONE goes to a gymï¿½.
Puts 5lbs worth of stress on the barbellsï¿½ and
walks out that same day, or one week later - looking
like Arnold Schwarzenegger!!  You must USE THAT
STRESS and add it to the 5lbsï¿½. then the 10lbsï¿½
then the 20lbsï¿½. then the 50lbs.  NO ONE gains

muscle mass without angst, pressure, the tug, the
pull, the agony of being dedicated to see some
positive result - otherwise, you wouldn't keep doing
it!!  That's what stress is forï¿½. It is NOT to
make us lose our hair and die of an early age.  Soo,
let's lose that fear-quotient that says, "THIS is
not for me!!"

The term, "White Fragility" is so amazing because it
is the polar opposite of what most Black people have
been suffering for lifetimes. We are not in love
with the idea and subject of race (either). We just
know that we are *suffering, cannot ever avoid it
completely, are tired of trying to be quiet and
complicit, and see so, so, so, so many affects that
this has upon our livesï¿½. Daily!!  So, when
someone brings up the subject of white fragilityï¿½.
We goï¿½ okay??????!!!!!?????

Later, I'll even discuss with you, why it's not good
to run away, or try to act like it's not thereï¿½
this is very similar to some of the things I've
already mentioned above, such as 'tapping out' or
pretending like you are not feeding yourself a
steady diet of lies. This has more to do with your
subconscious trying to do an even better job of
burying white fragility. There are of course health
aspects that can be affected within your body; for
example, have you ever thought about Schizophrenia??
I call Schizophrenia = an absence of truth,  So, I'm
curious to know by way of every readers experience -
Are Black people invisible to you??
But, I also want to help you see ï¿½ deep down
inside your subconscious, why you may have been
interpreting this nuanced feeling incorrectly.  The
subconscious mind (that hidden part of you) is
never, ever, ever out to hurt you.  But, it will
kick you a time or two to get your attentionï¿½.
Much like a nightmare after a midnight food fest
before going to bed. As human beingsï¿½ we are
pretty powerful, in that, we've been given so many
ways and opportunities to influence our own, and
sometimes, others lives.  But, do you think it's
fair that you should suffer (or in a term, NOT
SUFFER) such tiny fragile inconveniences, while

everyone else bears the grunt??!! ï¿½ If the shoe
were on the other footï¿½. You'd say ouch too!!

Soï¿½. Let's get into this - without the fear.
Let's start by jotting downï¿½ "What does White
Fragility mean to you??"  If you have an example or
storyï¿½ even better. They will prove tremendously
useful later.


SEPARATING INDIVIDUAL RACISM AND SYSTEMIC RACISM


There have been a couple of times when I've been
asked to speak publicly on racism; and most
certainly, I have also availed myself to my white or
foreign friends - in case they ever have questions.
And, I've even encouraged strangers "Go and seek out
a Black friend, with whom you can have these
discussions; Black people do not mind talking about
the subjectï¿½. So long as it's open and sincere.
They will also let you know it you've crossed the
line." Because, honestly speaking, that line could
be different for every person - and you should
respect their limits.  Otherwise, I often tell
people about amazing television shows that currently
air surrounding the subject of race, like critically
acclaimed, "Black-ish" - which talks about a new
generation growing in a completely different
environment then the one their parents grew up in,
but still maintaining those 'cultural Black truths'
that still apply regardless of who you are and where
you live. The Black experience is a very, very real
thingï¿½ and it's not a toy!

There's also a newer 2019 television show called:
"The Neighborhood" - starring Cedric The
Entertainer. The premise touches upon a successful
business owner in a predominantly Black community
(we'll call it, Pasadenaï¿½ hahah!!).  Then
gentrification pops up its head as a white family
moves next door. This white family is aware that
they are moving to a quaint little neighborhood that
slightly different from the one they just left, and

slightly more affordable too.  Well, the cultural
differences are vividly spelled out and placed in an
amazingly relatable, comical light. Being the only
white guy on the block sounds fun, right??!!  This
is an exceptional show, if I say so myself!!  You'll
also want to check out another show called:
[#FAM]ï¿½ï¿½  Short for family; and they are QUITE
the crew, graced by one of our living legends in
Sheryl Lee Ralph (famed - "Dreamgirls") and once
spicy teen from the 1960's Hit Movie, "A piece of
the Action" starring Bill Cosby & Sidney Poitierï¿½
and containing many other beloved now mega-famous
actors like James Earl Jones. So, as an easy
exercise in BLACK LIFESTYLE EXPOSURE, Hollywood may
slowly be changing, or should I say, we now have
black studio owners like Oprah Winfrey and Tyler
Perry, who are beginning to join forces with such
amazing Black directors as Ava DuVernay - of the
amazing movie: "Selma" - to create some of these new
and very excellent tv shows and movies. But, even
with that, there is absolutely no substitute for
actually being in the life of someone you truly care
about, who happens to be Black. The tv show - "This
is us" is great, but it's ON THE SCREEN. So, in
order for us all to learn and grow.... I implore you
to look at REAL LIFE.  And while you are looking at
life, know that there is a whole strategy around
keeping people separate, and making sure that
families are weakened by those others who feel that
HATE should have an advantage.


Recently, I saw a serious discussion about the
marketing strategies of some companies, and then I
saw a television parody about marketing to Black
people, and they both sounded strangely, eerily
similar. Take a glance for about a week at ads that
contain white people, vs. some ads that contain
Black people, and even those that contain both
parties. The ads containing both parties, will
typically have one Black guy amidst a group of white
males and females.  You will never find an ad where
it is the opposite. And, when we think of how this
is being programmed into our brains... it should

make you a little mad. Although some things have
gotten a little better, it is still a plot and a
ploy. So, when we think of white fragility, it is
very, very likely that - simple things like ads,
could be playing a game in your mind. If one grows
up with smokers on every side... how likely are you
to become a smoker yourself?? If you grow up with
people who are avid readers of books, do you believe
that you would grow up having an appreciation for
books (maybe - even more than the average joe who
reads). Take stock of what the mind sees.
Remember... there is no shut-off valve and the brain
works feverishly overtime to record every, single,
thing that it sees and hears. But... how do you
respond??


As we understand it, the subconscious mind is the
opposite of our very ordered, active, routine-loving
mind. No!! The subconscious seems at the least to be
centered around the idea of "risk". Things that are
new, as yet unlearned, or untapped, and most
definitely things that are more abstract or even
ideal seem to define what every human understands
this submerged portion of their minds to represent.
One can quickly imagine a child learning to ride a
bike for the first time. In most cases, you've seen
a bike beforeï¿½. You know there is joy to be had
there, but you have to figure out how to BALANCE
YOURSELF and hopefully not fall into the scary world
of scratched knees and bruised elbows - which may be
a little different then the previous courageous
years of learning to stand up or walk. There's no
way for any of us to definitively declare that for
one child to anotherï¿½. Those experiences are even
remotely similar.  Yet, the child (especially if
supported) will make the attempt. One foot onï¿½.
Another foot trying desperately to leave the ground,
and then there's the necessary speed to maintain
this new elevated position of riding.  So, as you
may imagineï¿½ where culture, and appreciation, and
acceptance of people whose life and choices are
different from yoursï¿½. This is like riding a bike
as a child - andï¿½.is a huge leap. If we could all

become transported back to our youths (with the
knowing cognitive mind that we have right now),
would then be able to truly attest to the real, very
real feelings we felt in that moment. Did you learn
to ride the first time or the twelfth time?? In
terms of memory recall, we may not even knowï¿½. But
our subconscious mind recorded the moment that we
DID actually ride WITH CONFIDENCE and/or without our
psychological training wheels. That is the sum total
job of the subconscious; adaptation and adjustment.

Now, to train yourself anew ï¿½ you will absolutely
have to become brutally honest with yourself; what
do you think about Black people, or the BLM
movement, or people who move into your neighborhood,
your work environment or company??

If the subconscious were just a matter of clicking a
button or snapping your finger.... there are some
who would still 'fake understanding'. This is why
your discomfort is so important.
Fill in the QUESTION marks and complete the
sentence: QUESTION/STATEMENT: I have discomfort
surrounding.....??

Take for example, nervous laughter; is that
something that feels like discomfort for you??
Maybe you have a discomfort with being touched or
hugged?? As we have already jotted down what white
fragility means to you, now we want to get even more
specific. Perhaps your trigger is more subject
related, where you feel something as it relates to
jobs, driving in traffic, taking orders from a Black
man or woman, however. How do you resolve those ill
feelings when you are in the moment. Record your
thoughts -- thoughts of murder, furious anger,
breaking things, headaches with aspirin, take a long
walk?? We need to know about these as well - in
order to nudge healing.  ON a scale of 1 to 100....
how much, or to what percentage do you feel you OWN
white fragility??  #1 / 1% being = I can solve my
problem in a month.... or #100 / 100% being = I have
hatred that seems irreversible and I may need
therapy. So, as we get closer to these... it seems
(to me) that white fragility has the potential to

make one feel non-existent *(or invisible) in the
feeling and acknowledgement space. It's as if [WF]
has two faces... one is public, and one is private.
Neither desire to emote outwardly, but depending
upon the crack in one's subconscious, it comes
bubbling up out of nowhere ... yet, it's hard to
perceive = like a faucet that has an occasional
drip. Another thing could be... "explaining away".
Where this is pretty common among many white people
who desire to be know-it-alls... or, who are rigid
in their nature, they will repeat what you said as a
question.  If you say, "I'm going to run over you
with my car!!" - they will try to 'explain away'
what they think you said, but without acknowledging
the fact that they have made you mad. They will NOT
own it. They retort, "If I'm hearing you
correctly... it seems like you're saying that
something is not right, and it's affecting you to
the point of losing control of your vehicle??!!"
This dig that we are requesting has many faces, both
in the feeling and communicating areas of yourself,
but are probably masked over by daily duties, by
avoidance, by keeping your distance, or making
jokes, or maybe shows up in the actual foods you
eat. We want you to discover all of those that my
apply to you specifically, and subjectively. Is
there something you would like to talk about, but
are not giving yourself permission??  Is there
something that you watch (or don't watch) on tv
which makes you feel a certain amount of annoyance??
Let's uncover as many as we can.


DEMOGRAPHIC NEIGHBORHOODS


In today's world, we derive a lot of our information
from statistics and information that is presented to
us through our news media. Now more than ever, we
are able to see various climates of people
throughout the world and even see glimpsed portions
of how they might actually live.

In the coming sections, I want to tackle the idea of
demographics as it relates to neighborhoods and
numbers,  and as well, I would love to also discuss
television and the perceptions that we apply when we
are watching television and/or thinking about people
of color as it relates to television programming.

Often, we say that art imitates life. And, no more
is that true then in the hit television show
"SHAMELESS". The still running 8 season television
show "Shameless" is hilarious - as it focuses upon
the trials of a South Side Chicago family.  And
although this series represents the [opposite of
fragility], with all of its outlandishly
dysfunctional issues, the family wins.  Just the
fact that they are a "WHITE" Southside Chicago
family is brilliantly unique, and yet, there is
still some reality to its themes. The show *(at
times) even stands up for equality!!! Short-lived
protests, arguments, or dialogue that, while against
privilege, is obviously mocked by the fact that this
featured family IS WHITE.  Upon regularly seeing
these characters, you start to notice the pattern of
how this tv family (almost on-purpose) make
themselves the target of so many common poverty
ills, such as - abuse, drugs, jail, poor judgment,
fighting, poor life management skills - where they
can barely keep the heat and the lights on, all
fabricated from the root of  - parental negligence.

Yet, somehow ï¿½ they bounce back!! They remain
resilient.  And, at times, they even stick together.
Oh, and don't worryï¿½. their beloved Black little
baby brother [Liam] is always carefully dangling at
the edge of their very distracted, collective,
periphery. The show is great!! The question becomes:
How else would any one live on the Southside if
that's the real, factual, reality for any and every
family that lives there?? It's a mystery and a
sweeping generalization. It's also comically
opposite its typical dramatic urban rival: "The
Chi".

There's no denying that people draw up conclusions
about 'good neighborhoods' and 'bad neighborhoods',

ï¿½ or good places to go and bad places to go,
ï¿½.or good schools and bad schools. We all do it -
or should I say, we all "by into it".
There is no denying that there is a major disparity
between the lifestyle and experiences of white
people versus the lifestyle and experiences of black
people. And, when discussing the subject of Racism,
White Superiority, White Fragility,  White
Privilege, and the like ï¿½ all of these various
titles become the hotbed that is easily situated and
seated under the subject of racism or racial
disparity.

I bring the show 'Shameless' up in detail for
several reasons. The main reason being - if it were
a show centered around a black family in that part
of town and in those conditions, no one would watch
It!!  It wouldn't be funny.  It would be a
stereotype.  In fact the show would never have been
made it all!! But, when we place a 'white family' in
that part of town, under those conditionsï¿½. It's a
HIT TV SERIES!! You place a white family in those
conditions, mind you, the very same South Chicago
area that you hear about on the news, with all of
the random shootings, and the murder rate that is
(according to every news channel) "through the roof"
and completely out of control - SUDDENLY, you go
from shaking your head in disgust to laughter.  We
make light of it, and we avoid it ï¿½simultaneously.
We try to reason it away by sayingï¿½ "It's a tv
show; it's not real".  And even still, the
Gallagher's just make it look so damn livable and
fun to watch.

No doubt, (I'm saying) If you watch the show and
this family you might learn a few things ï¿½ like
how an interracial couple can really, truly love
each other. You get to see him shower his beautiful
black wife with love, appreciation, respect, and so
much admiration. This is just an example!!
Otherwiseï¿½. Aside from its brilliant moments, this
show's theme and carefully crafted, crass subject
matter flies high and free in the face of all that
America consistently uses AGAINST black people. Tv

(like this) can force our perceptions to become even more unconsciously biased.

Every single facet of the show is so over-the-topï¿½. but possible!!!  Many of the dilemmas presented can easily represent something that any African American person could live through as part of their daily plight. On tv, we laugh at it!!  We don't always equate that that is (could be) someone's real life. We watch it (someone's reality) played out weekly ï¿½.for several seasons now!! And NO, I am not asserting that the show should be taken off of the air; the show is great!  I'm just highlighting the fact that America has some truly amazing double standards. How is it that (again), - If we kept everything the same ï¿½and made the Gallagher family, a black family, the Show would be shunned and frowned upon. IMAGINE NOW: A black father willingly ï¿½and yes, I do mean to overstate, "willingly and willfully" neglecting his 6 kids. A Black father doing drugs in front of his 6 children, teaching them to lie and steal on his behalf. In fact, someone reading these words will most undoubtedly say, ï¿½"That's possible; that's real life" ï¿½."That's already happening"ï¿½.. "sounds pretty typical to me!!"  And, I am saying that THAT point alone, it is the preferred brush we used to paint all of black families. Ironically, Unbeknownst to most white people, that kind of father is overwhelmingly and largely NOT the kind of father that you would find throughout the predominantly Black householdï¿½. But, your perception of that show would certainly challenge you to think otherwise. Most Black people are nothing like The Gallagher's.

The Gallagher's [who always are] rising to the occasion, making a way-out-of-no-way, who despite each sour event turn those lemons into the most delicious lemonade you've ever tasted in your lifeï¿½ They win!! The WHITE PEOPLE win again!! Ooh, that beautiful 45 minute TV world where the stress is magically gone away and/or is resolved where everyone is smiling at the end. Yetï¿½.., if I may force the issue, most [white] people would never

take into their own personal consideration that kind
of daily relenting stress and trauma as common, in
the way that some black people may have to endure it
-- living in poverty.  We guiltlessly watch that
program and then ï¿½ turning our heads awayï¿½.fast
forward to your very next encounter with a person of
color who may need your help -- and you will muster
yourself to have zero empathy for help you could
easily provide for that person of color. Be it:
consideration, a kind word, a small act of
generosity, or how about some basic human
appreciation and respect. You quickly forget,
despite the fact that the ones who are actually
going through the EXACT SAME THING that you have
just finished watching on television - is standing
directly in front of you (in different form). But,
luckilyï¿½ you are not obliged, and don't have to
care or be concerned either way. In our perceptions,
in our subconscious mind, we train ourselves to not
care since it's not affecting us.

Our racist tendencies have several masks. And,
ï¿½although I am NOT SAYING that people who enjoy
the show are racist, I am saying we need to be
careful of are two-faced-ness. We need to more
closely observe how this system is set up against
people of color or more readily feel the unjust
differences in weight and measurements that ARE
being applied because someone is white and/or comes
from a different area than you.  Prejudice is a
precursor of racism.

If all things were truly considered equal then we
wouldn't be having this discussion at all.  But, as
it stands, we have as recently as March 2019 - as I
mentioned prior - found a spotlight cast upon bribes
that have been paid for college admissions by dozens
of people.  Namely, as it has been publicized, the
'MEDIA FACES OF THE GUILTY' that we have seen are
that of: Lori Loughlin And Felicity Huffman.  I
assert again, If all things were considered equal
then getting into a prestigious college would be
based upon ones past high school grades. If there is
worthy educational merit present, that would allow
ANY student to enter the college of their choice

based upon traditional college performance Standards, right??!!??  But here, we have bribes that have been paid in the amount of $500,000 by dozens of people, ï¿½.seemingly, all in Hollywood; ï¿½.all white, ï¿½.all of sizeable wealth.

This also further plays into the subconscious stereotype that Black kids from poor Black areas (like the South Side of Chicago) cannot afford certain types of colleges, even though they may outperform scholastically, all of their white counterparts. Systemically, white people seemingly crave advantage, craving better schools, better neighborhoods,  better economic status - and at the heart of thisï¿½. There's nothing wrong with any of these things - SO LONG as it does not "DEPRIVE" another person of the exact same opportunity.

In this instance, we really believe that these people are guilty of bribes. And, even though we know it's wrong to lie and to bribe, yetï¿½ somehow we are able to turn a blind eye.  Blatant proof!! It would seem that white people LOVE to ignore truth!! Even If nowhere else but in his presidency alone, we have often heard President trump make several untrue accusations. Yet we deny actually hearing anything at all. There seems to be no level playing field for anyone.  And anything is fair gain so long as you don't get caught.

Despite the fact that It is estimated that Trump has lied in the amount of 8000+ times (and we refuse to believe him or call him a liar) yet, In that same breath we have Actresses Felicity Huffman and also Lori Loughlin - who were charged with college entrance scams. We believe their guilt more than the other.

These women (and dozens of others) wanted to ensure that their children got into the 'best schools' by paying their way as opposed to their children earning the right grades to get into the school. As I stated before, there are actually a whole, publicly published list of people who have done this; seemingly from Hollywood; seemingly white

professionals; seemingly people who have wealth and
can afford to pay an extra $500,000 bribe for their
children to secretly, privately, and undeservedly
enter into prestigious schools.

You'll also want to note that Huffman's
husband/Actor: William H Macy - plays the extremely
delinquent and negligent father in the
aforementioned hit TV show "Shameless".  So here, we
find that art imitating life plays out so well in
finding that William H Macy's wife Actress Felicity
Huffman Is now trying to pay her way into a
prestigious school on behalf of her children (is NOT
unlike an episode of 'Shameless' where (Black
brother) 'Liam' is recruited because of his skin
color.

This is not white Fragility but it is absolutely
white privilege. So even though it's something that
will benefit your children directly, you can see how
adversely speaking or conversely speaking, this does
not benefit every child nor does it benefit black
children. Why is it that you get to pay to have your
child go to a prestigious school while the black
child doesn't get that same opportunity?! And, I'm
sure many people will argue, "well it's because
she's an actress and she makes more money. She
should be able to do with that money whatever she
wants"!!  The problem in that statement is ONE WORD:
WHATEVER.  To make such a glib, partially thought-
out statement would be completely missing the point:
White Privilege says that it's OK for me to do
whatever I want - so long as I'm not caught. While
White Fragility usually wants to dismiss having the
discussion about racially charged principles and
equality altogether.


AMAZING BLACK TV SHOWS AND MOVIES OF BLACK DIRECTORS


In this century, it has become even more clear that
black directors, black filmmakers, black writers in
Hollywood emphatically and absolutely need to be

more concerned about making its own stories. Stories
created by black people. We realize that the
narratives are already against us, but what,
actively, are we doing to counter that?

Just as I have mentioned several television shows
above in the previous section. This section even
more so, highlights the fact that we are on the cusp
of many, new, cutting edge shows that feature black
families, black lives, and black entertainment in a
more positive manner. We are now feeling the need,
in the present, to move away from urban thugs and
gang related stories - to tell stories that speak of
Hope; stories that speak of excellence; and stories
that delve more deeply into the actual factual
reality that black people live on a daily basis and
not just the ones that we wanna see portrayed on the
screen.  In reality, black families especially from
the late 1950s and 1960s moving forward, have been
very whole - in terms of their relationships to one
another. There was not a lot of fighting, there was
not a lot of abuse, there was not a lot of crime and
criminal mentality.  But, you can say that there is
a lot of feuding whenever it came to white people
and say... urban development, which in today's
society carries the name: gentrification. Seeing
[WF] in the midst of all these climates, will lessen
the strength of the root growing in the future.

Growing up in a black family, It is expressly taught
that you will represent your family, in that, you
will exceed those people who gave birth to you. Now,
this theme is common throughout families as a whole,
regardless of racial backgrounds. But there are
certain triggers that are more adequately
represented within the black family - because It
serves as thread throughout all of your life, on how
you should be treated, how you should conduct
yourself, and how far and how high you can achieve
your own success. And, with the onset of black
media, black salesï¿½. we are starting to now hold
the paintbrush and control the stroke that we would
like to see portrayed.

KILL BLACK MALE TENDERNESS / KEEP THEM WEAK


In a sentence, Black men are always the monster.
Monsters who don't support or love their family.
So, with that narrative... the command is to keep
the black man weak, and to keep the Black man down.
Bind the strong man... and you can have the whole
house.  White fragility is terrified to take a
stance on this... at least, not audibly and out in
the open public. So, we ask... how would you like to
change that?? Or, are you content within white
fragility to keep stepping on the neck of black men
in order to keep some similitude of comfort and
supposed peace??  How can one battling white
fragility show appreciation towards the black man,
and his family who needs him [alive]?? Such
questions are hard... and may not find an easy place
to land - but are worth pushing for, even as it
relates to your own personal healing of white
fragility. Towards the conclusion of this book, we
hope that you will better understand your own
personal role and maybe even your own (unconscious
and) implicit biases that seek such outworn arrogant
ego approval. In essence, we need ALL FAMILIES to be
whole in America, [period].


THE FUTURE OF SENSITIVITY


As time moves forward, and bad things continue to
happenï¿½.. There is a level of sensitivity that
will be foisted upon the unsuspecting world. Much
like the #METOO movement, BLM movement, Gender
Equality movement, and many more as yet unforeseen
issues, and many other as yet unknown provocative
events surface - when THAT "something" happens and
the weights of public opinion are placed on the
balanceï¿½.. "EASILY OFFENDED" is going to be the
'super-norm' and like a deadly and fatal paper cut,
when it used to be a trip to the guillotine. We are
becoming "overly sensitive" in the wrong wayï¿½.. As
opposed to [like we are purporting in this book]

using your mind, and your sensitivity, and your
background, to try to UNDERSTAND AND APPRECIATE
things that deeply affect us all. Thus, we don't
want anyone left behind.


NEGATIVE ASSUMPTIONS


I personally think that when you try to change
something (blindly) or when we try to act-like-we-
know-something, it is potentially dangerous. YES, it
may be true that you can change your habits after 31
days of very consistent effort, but, that may only,
mostly, or particularly be true because it is
extremely subjective; it affects Y.O.U. more than it
affects someone else near-to-you (emotionally
connected to you, your heart, and soul). Thus, as we
have already talked about BELIEFS - I'm asking you
to check your beliefs as they relate to others and
people we attract to ourselves. Consciously picking
something to nurture within ourselves - like
planting a seed in a garden - you more or less know
what to expect: JOY, LOVE, FORGIVENESSï¿½ what you
don't know is HOW AND WHEN IT WILL COME TO YOU.  So,
in looking at 'negative assumptions' (especially as
it relates to race), you boobytrap yourself and your
connections to people of color, againï¿½ possibly
because you think that you-think-you-know!!

When you make a negative assumption towards a Black
person, for example, regardless of how genuine you
TRY to beï¿½. You send that Black man or woman into
a [fight / flight] position. That Black man or woman
will look at you with immediate suspicion and/or
close themselves off, or shut down to reciprocating
with the white person in the equation. I'll give you
an easy example, that I actually may have touched
upon before in previous pages. EXAMPLE: Upon finding
yourself in the space or attention of a Black man or
womanï¿½. You quickly greet them and express that
greeting as:  "What's up?!!" -- Notice that I have
not said that this person / these people are
strangers to each other.  To assert the greeting
"what's up?!!" is reserved for someone you know

very, very, well. It is an ethnic cultural
appropriation. So, with the new understanding that
you are NOT considered a "friend" to this Black
person, you come off as a joke or someone who is
trying to "make a joke" at that person's expense.
And largelyï¿½. depending upon what comes next or
what is next said, you may unwittingly be calling
for a (real) physical fight.  There's an assertion
of audacity that is NOT going to be met with
peacemaking.  This is also true for the N-word.

But, in this next example, let's make it a co-worker
(two people who see each other every day), not a
total stranger.  You can guess for yourself right
now, how that might play outï¿½.. Yet, in this
scenario - as opposed to the above scenario, there
are many more outcomes in-between that initial
greeting and the next statement. Even if you mean to
merely be polite and culturally consciousï¿½. You
still could cause a shift in that Black person's
disposition, mood, or internal psyche (NOTE: this is
NOT to say that every single Black person is
adversely trigger-hyper-sensitiveï¿½ instead, they
have just trained themselves over decades and
exponential life experiences - to sense, discern,
observe and not put up with insults, slights,
disingenuousness, and even hatred, racism, or
bigotry).  What I'm saying is, we actually pick up
on these like a radar!! AND THUS, you may have (now)
created a moment whereby that person of color may
never feel they can trust you at work or in work
related situations; you may have accidentally caused
[them] to look unprofessional, or as if they're
being forced to be viewed (perceived) in an
unprofessional manner!! ï¿½And I hear you, "Wellï¿½
that wasn't my intent at all, Oh my gosh!!!"  To
thatï¿½ I'd again say, "THIS IS WHY we wrote the
book!!"

Take as a parallel example, someone who constantly,
abruptly, or publicly is complimenting a womanï¿½.
Any womanï¿½. And yes, even a Black woman who IS the
consummate professional, who has her attire
together, is beautiful, has her business 'thinking'
cap on, who is known for and is successfully

striving for her corporate goals (or otherwise); you
WILL offend them.  This piggy-backs on the #METOO
movement, where we've had habitual abusers like
Harvey Weinstein, egregiously take advantage of
females in Hollywood - for decades!!  It is this
kind of taboo that many Black people will defiantly
(and/or suffering quietly) SHUN. Black people know -
there's a time and a place for everythingï¿½. And we
have NOT given you the green light to defame us in
public or at work. Again, "What's up?!!" is a
cultural greeting that should be left to us. ï¿½.If
we like you, we'll probably say it first (but it
does not in any way erase other distinctions - like
Mr., Ms., Mrs., Sir or Ma'am). Get to know "us" [the
Black HUMAN PERSON], ï¿½first.


AGENT OF CHANGE


You may not want to changeï¿½. But if you DO want to
change, and you understand the implications of
horrendous acts, beliefs, and twisted logics
surrounding the historically ill treatment of people
of African descent and African-American people who
were otherwise savagely transplanted (into this
American construct as a nation) - you must sincerely
desire to change whatever lingering ideologies that,
given the fact that most citizen of the USA are NOT
indigenous, these ideologies are still
inappropriately embedded in one's belief systemï¿½
and dare I say, MUST BE PURGED!! There's nothing
divisive or harmful required, other than a stark and
cutting contrast from what you formerly believe to a
completely different and new open-minded belief =
and one that allows you, or anyone, to look at
another with appreciation, and not disgust, disdain,
or intolerance.  It's actually holistically more
healthy. And so, we invite you - even at the end of
this book to free yourself.  White fragility is a
decided, conscious, alert and alarm system - that
has worked to keep you separate from others who will
more than likely enrich your life.  It's not enough
anymore to take a trip and feel like you've gotten

to know a culture, country, or people - if you have
not spent ANY time with them.  It only proves to
show that your world is really small... and ready to
be overthrown by the rest of us who seek universal
and collective goodness.  Take the steps... make the
leap.... HEAL!!


March 24, 2019
.... After publishing this book, I definitely plan
to go to Youtube (as a momentary, fun, comparison)
to hear Dr. Robin Di'Angelo speak about her book.
Likewise, it would be amazing to see how everyone is
moving forward within themselves. But, as for now...
I am just going to rejoice with you all for having
taken the journey with me. Let's hope that there are
others who desire to step into the light of "white
fragility completely healed".


 Star Trek 2021

I think anyone would agree that working towards
"healing" is a noble effort and fundamentaly
worthwhile - if not healthy. But, there is, I
believe a psychological aspect to healing that only
surfaces within the individual. A form of joy, as it
were, that bubbles up into the belief system that
people hold - and sometimes whether correctly or
incorrectly informs their actions. This feeds into
the very beginning of the book - which eludes to
upbringing and examining oneself to discover whether
you're an alien that did not birth from a woman's
womb. Beyond that, is this notion that, if you are
NOT an alien.... then (in the words of Star Trek),
we don't need to further consider whether you are
'Federation human' or Klingon?? But.... I contest
here (sadly), that we do still need to address these
Klingon-like humanoids that are just now beginning
to reveal themselves - namely, "Trump Supporters".

As I type this addition to the end of this book and
any subsequent discussion that is extremely likely,
we have NOW elected a new 46th President of the
United States: Joseph Robinette Biden Jr.  But,

alongside the dancing in the street, we have our
current golfing President Trump - who has no plans
to leave the WH. Trump, who HAS NOT even called to
concede nor congratulate the new president elect for
his narrowly yet graciously won victory. And, just
as there are people dancing in the streets, there
are people newly protesting the American vote and
the voting system at large as directed by the
leader, touting and demanding lawsuits, childishly
ranting to the point that he and others chant to:
stop the vote -or- count the vote (as they feel the
election was stolen from our current WH resident).
It begs the question, "what are these people's
reality and what is going on in their subconscious
that they don't see or want to acknowledge the very
obvious difference between these two administrative
styles??" I quietly argue that it further reveales
the Klingon-like evil interests and intentions of
everyday people.... and those people who seek to
enlist real physical harm. It is a new topic and
subject on shows like Bill Mahr and other -- that 70
million people voted FOR EVIL, or more generally
speaking... voted for 4 more years of chaos,
notwithstanding that there may have been some
amazing things that may have been accomplished by
this person in the White House. But, we cannot ever
ignore his racist rants, radical tweets, incendiary
comments against Muslim people, Black people, LatinX
people, and the list goes on and on and on and on.
It would seem today that politics is "SUPPOSED" to
outshine one's character and the constructive tenets
that everyone should have already learned - such as
the perfectionistic idea of loving your neighbor as
yourself. The USA has indoctrinated a commencement
and movement [of and for] people who do NOT believe
in civility (it seems). How did that happen???
Again, I cite the purpose of this book as being an
aid to answer that question.

White Fragility in and of itself is a worthy cause
to challenge, but I'm sure you can see the immediate
relevance that extends the concept of acceptance,
wholeness, righteousness, and even politically
correctness which should permeate today's climate.
Of course, anyone can vote for whomever they

choose.... but, what I'm getting at is - the idea
that your vote and/or candidate should encite you to
more hatred then before. Let's look at a couple of
things regarding the Black vote.

Since the election of former President Barack Obama,
Black people have become a tiny bit more
disenfranchised with America and the overall process
to the point that we did not turn out to vote in the
2016 election. And, even if we had... we almost
unanimously WOULD NOT have voted for Trump .....
why, you ask??? ....Because, we don't easily forget.
We have long held Trump as a racist when we began to
hear the truths that Donald J. Trump the real estate
mogul:

- Would not rent to people of color as far back the
  1960's.
- Took out a full page ad calling for the death
  penalty of what is now called the 'Exonerated
  Five'. Five innocent Black youths of NYC.
- Has a parent lineage tied to the KKK

And these are just some of the pre-election things
that you hear floating about that highlight his very
poor and narcissistic character. And, we were
quickly proven correct as we later learned about the
plethora of tweets, comments, etc - throughout his
tenure. Things that should never be mentioned among
a world leader. We recall his platform points and
his base supporters - all aligning to give a
critical mass birth to people aspirations (not just
complaints), that White America is again "ALL
IMPORTANT". His now very famous slogan: "Make
America Great Again" -- not even subtle, became a
rallying cry for all who could these ideas within
themselves as 'proper, right, and good'. It becomes
a scary notion, that.... in the face of the American
Ideal, we have chosen someone who diametrically
opposes the originally inclusive and
constitutionally sound theme of 'the Great American
Melting Pot'. Instead.... he replaced that historic
legacy with:

- "Shithole Countries"

- "Grab them by the pussy" female reference
- "Go back to where you came from" - rhetoric
- His - US Military (deaths) as suckers and losers
- His extremely incorrect and incorrigible
  declaration that "I've done more for the Black
  community than Abraham Lincoln"
- His - "It is what it is" twisted slang regarding
  the (now) 250K+ deaths of the pandemic
- "Liberate Michigan" (and other similar tweets)
  energizing the foiled potential kidnapping of
  Michigan's public official
- His blind ignorance that "I'm the least racist
  person in the room" retorts
- Not to mention policies whereby 545 children were
  separated from their parents at the Mexican-
  American border (and caged)

.....and so many other things that it would take me
all day to list them all. History will not be able
to sidestep these atrocities emanating from a
sitting president, let alone the potential for
collusion, political misconduct, Republican party
silence and aquiescence, and more. It will be
totally incumbent upon an individual, and a purpose-
filled society to look back in hindsight an learn
better - for our collective future. These
individuals will, in fact, be much like the voyagers
of Star Trek - who seek out new worlds and new
civilizations.... but, starting right here and now -
on planet Earth. These individuals will be people
who are not dead-set on destroying themselves and
the people around them. These people will be
fighting - just as African-Americans have been
fighting since the inception of this country and
slavery - to gain freedom from such tyrannies;
fighting to merely exist!! These people will find it
necessary to deport themselves in such a high and
honorable manner so as not to bolster civil war, all
while having the right to defend themselves against
marauders and interlopers. These people are you...
the readers of this book.

And so, you see the very real and very active now-
do-well agenda that this book's healing inserts.
Absolutely, your first battlelines against White

Fragility will take you farther than you can
imagine, but it is NOT the end of the journey as
these pages might suggest. No... to the contrary!!
Think of the chapters we've already tackled. For
example, the theme of #NOT_TAPPING_OUT -- Black
people have not given up on freedom; we have not
given up on the idea of restoration (even after 400
years); we have not lost sight of the fact that we
have built this country; we have not lost the vision
of the American Dream. We have NOT given up....
'though, sometimes it feels like that is the best
thing we could do. We are convinced that once we are
okay... the whole of America will be okay. That's
almost parabolic if you think of it: "A chain is
only as strong as its weakest link" -- in that, any
people group who stands at the brink of extinction,
must needs to be rescued, restored, and returned to
a place of health. That includes people suffering
from White Fragility, White Supremacy, or implicit
biases. We can no longer pretend that things or
history (as it were) is a foregone conclusion, but a
foundational springboard to launch from.


Amendment November 8th, 2020

The rest of this year, for those of you who are
blessed to be reading this book, will playout like a
terrain map - which should lead to a magical
treasure, but not without a few perils along the
way. If there are perils, we sincerely hope on this
day that they will be few. Since none of us have a
crystal ball, we will needs to be vigilant. We will
actively celebrate people, events, groups set in
movement, and endorse peace. We will teach and talk
about this to our children.

It is my most sincere hope that - you will prosper,
EVEN AS YOUR SOUL PROPSPERS!!

If there have ever been an interest in animals at
the brink of extinction, we must NOW add ourselves
to that list in seeing that there is much, much work
to be done. I only wish to scare you into action. It
would be great if the notion of this book were

merely conjecture, and not one of existential
exegesis (as it were) - we could just think
ourselves into a better form. But, the instructions
that have been left for you in this book - are
overriding in that you must see yourself actively
completing its instructions - with results. To walk
away from this book with a more reinforced feeling
of 'whiteness' would only serve as an angering
distraction to witness a retroactive regression of
oneself - to an infantile time when you were
breastfed and handled as someone incapable of
evolving on your own.

In another book, I actually talk about our 'womb
environment' as it relates to - being outside of the
womb and finding / aligning yourself with people
with whom you can find nuture and support. This is
NOT co-dependency!! I am trying to highlight the
aspect of life that give you 'choices'.
Understanding, when we use that muscle correctly and
actively.... you find yourself living out
experiences that could not have happened on a normal
mundane Tuesday. You open yourself to your higher
self - awaiting you.

Every human being is laced with DNA that suggests
that no man is an island. Every human being desires
to be 'connected' -- and seeing how we all come from
one species, it is widely yet silently held that we
should all stand together to represent the best of
who we are; we seek to improve ourselves. Small
ideosyncrasies either flare up or cool down our
angst to understand and/or be understood - and we,
like a headache, seek such an operationally societal
aspirin to assuage any discomfort that comes because
you either feel or imagine that another is against
you based upon some tiny difference as the choicest
flavor of your favorite coffee. We would hope that
NO ONE is that petty!! Yet, on so many fronts, and
in our current climate.... we witness many minor
grievances turning into lofe-death situations that
should never have occurred... or arisen.
#Defund_the_Police became a popular montra after the
deaths of George Floyd & Breonna Taylor -- because
they represent this very thought. Police, whose job

it is to "protect & serve" their particular
communities have turned into vigilantes whose
scared-for-their-lives perceptions somehow cannot
muster the ability to de-escalate any event within
their jurisdiction. They patrol areas with a bias;
they arrest people sitting quietly in coffe shops.
For, on a daily basis, they forfeit their human DNA
to rebuild themselves into a enemy-soldier-like
personas who can't relate anymore. And, it is this
point that I'd like to highlight as well, much like
an aforementioned comment regarding Black people's
hatred of white people; it's a misnomer.  But,
regarding the police, who were indeed created to
capture slaves.... conversely speaking, Black people
want to be safe to -- safe from the people. The
police who have broken their constitutional oaths to
treat and capture like animals, anyone who
brandishes Black or Brown skin. And, although we've
tolerated and lives with the very same fear that
they have concocted for themselves.... we have for
generations upon generations actually lived the fear
they claim to face. Being hung from trees, as recent
as 2020 in areas of California and the South. Yet,
we hold fast to our humanity!! Black people
consciously and very instinctually refuse to
abjectly deny our human DNA -- in fact, how could we
??

It takes a concerted effort to deny that - and it
takes a concerted effort to hate that same or any
person.  Hatred of hair styles, is not real; hatred
of clothing is not real; hatred of a living being IS
REAL. And to use any amount of authority (in a
hateful or spiteful manner) is both insidious, and
extremely morally deficient. One cannot command and
demand 'his/her' authority as being real, without
hold that authority in proper context. Otherwise, it
is autocratically hostile.

Individual power is such that one contains oneself
within reasonable meaning and usages. You develop
power and purpose via your viewpoint and your
actions - which should remain consistent with your
core. We don't expect a child to come out of teh
womb driving a car, or speaking any language

fluently. And so, this walk away from white
fragility is sprinkled with opportunities to course
correct, inspire, and even admonish any onlooker who
defies to contest that you are NOT authentic, are
NOT holding something substantive and vital. It is
the practice of both looking inward and looking
outward - to calibrate what best poses as a humane
and human.

I have instructed you to be "UP FRONT" and I have
instructed you to further explore the fictitious
university and its various departments in order to
discover what is most subjectively circumspect as it
relates to your world. You are now equipped with
more than enough amunition to wage war on white
fragility. No doubt, you will be victorious. You
have already done a great deal of work - just by
getting to the end of this read. If there are others
for whom you a great love or respect, we leave you
with a fertile seed ready for the planting.

The years ahead  await us all.




The End

www.ingramcontent.com/pod-product-compliance
Lightning Source LLC
Chambersburg PA
CBHW031918270726
48655CB00006BA/2540